D0362030

THE OFFICIAL
SURVIVAL
GAME
MANUAL

Most Pocket Books are available at special quantity discounts for bulk purchases for sales promotions, premiums or fund raising. Special books or book excerpts can also be created to fit specific needs.

For details write the office of the Vice President of Special Markets, Pocket Books, 1230 Avenue of the Americas, New York, New York 10020.

THE OFFICIAL
SURVIVAL
GAME
MANUAL

Text and Photos by

LIONEL ATWILL

PREFACE BY CHARLES GAINES

PUBLISHED BY POCKET BOOKS NEW YORK

For Elena and Amanda

Photographs and line drawings by Lionel Atwill

Another *Original* publication of POCKET BOOKS

 POCKET BOOKS, a division of Simon & Schuster, Inc.
1230 Avenue of the Americas, New York, N.Y. 10020

Copyright © 1983 by The Survival Game, Inc.
Preface copyright © 1983 by Charles Gaines

All rights reserved, including the right to reproduce
this book or portions thereof in any form whatsoever.
For information address Pocket Books, 1230 Avenue
of the Americas, New York, N.Y. 10020

ISBN: 0-671-47395-6

First Pocket Books printing June, 1983

10 9 8 7 6 5 4 3 2 1

POCKET and colophon are registered trademarks
of Simon & Schuster, Inc.

Printed in the U.S.A.

CONTENTS

PLAYING THE GAME

WHY, WHERE AND WOW!

PREFACE
By Charles Gaines

One night during the spring of 1976 or 1977, Hayes Noel and I were grilling a king mackerel and drinking gins and tonic on the patio of a house in Jupiter Island, Florida. While we were grilling and drinking we talked, as we often do, about play. We both believe in play. Specifically, in this ginny conversation, we began to construct from an idea of Hayes's a form of play that might contain the childhood exhilaration of stalking and being stalked, might call on a hodgepodge of instincts and skills and might allow as wide a variety of responses as possible to this rich old question: How do I get from where I am now to where I want to be?

Well, the Survival Game was conceived *in utero* that night—conceived as a lark, as something that was fun to think about. Somehow we kept thinking about it, discussing it, always in the context of other forms of fun, in New York City, on Martha's Vineyard, in a duck blind off the New Hampshire coast with Richie White and Carl Sandquist, and in dozens of places with Bob Gurnsey, who damned near would have quit smoking to have guaranteed the healthy birth of the idea. In short, over the course of a couple of years, we all "swole up," as they say down south, with the possibilities. George Butler found the gun in a catalog. Gurnsey and Noel and I invented rules. In a prenatal rush, we found land, planned weekend parties around the birth, picked the original players, named judges and bought booze and camo grease paint—and we had a hell of a good time doing all of it. We had an even better time actually bringing the Survival Game into the world on a Saturday afternoon in June 1981 in Henniker, New Hampshire. And

7

after that there was the fun of continuing to play, of refining the Game, of the party weekends surrounding it, of introducing new people to it and finding that almost all of them loved it—and also, admittedly, of seeing it written about and televised.

Now, largely because of Bob Gurnsey's efforts, the Survival Game is a business, and people all over the place are playing it. There is this fine book about it, by Lionel Atwill. A song has been written about it, and someone in California owns the movie rights. All that didn't happen simply because the Game was fun to think about and later to play, though it was precisely that fun which made everything that happened later meaningful to Hayes Noel and Bob Gurnsey and myself. All of it happened, I believe, because the Survival Game extends itself naturally into a number of universally interesting metaphors. Playing the Game can actually show you in its own terms who you are, and there is no more interesting metaphor than that. The Game can also be seen as a metaphor for the efficacy of teamwork, for universal cause and effect and for the manner in which consequences evolve from sequential decisions. And some people will even tell you that it is a sure and ugly metaphor for war. We don't believe that is so, but I am not out to argue the point here.

The Game may be *interesting* because of these various metaphorical extensions, but it is not fun because of them; it is fun simply because it is fun. Conceived as a lark, it is a lark to play—an intricate, demanding and thrilling child's play which, like all the best games, can never be played perfectly. Play like that for adults is always in short supply. With this book you can have fun reading about the Survival Game. Then you can have the great good fun of going out and playing it.

WELCOME TO THE NATIONAL SURVIVAL GAME

1

PLAYING FOR FUN

Forget baseball and football. Forget basketball, hockey, tennis and golf. Forget skateboards, wind surfing, hopscotch, and Hula-Hoops.

"Bang, you're dead!" is our National Sport.

It takes many forms: cowboys and Indians, cops and robbers, good guys and bad guys and, more recently, the likes of Starsky and Hutch. Between the ages of four and twelve everyone stalks a friend—cap gun, water pistol or bent stick in hand—and, with palms sweating, mouth drying and pulse quickening, gets the drop on him or her and says those magic words:

"Bang, you're dead!"

But little boys graduate to more elaborate games—football or Pac-Man.

And most little girls are weaned away by the parental notion that little girls shouldn't *do* such things.

By the age of pimples, "Bang, you're dead!" has, for most of us, died a quiet death, yet in our guts we remember the thrill.

Now that thrill has been resurrected in an adult form that challenges a player's guile, intellect, nerves and stamina. It is called the Survival Game, and damn near everyone who plays it wants to play it again. And again. And again.

There are variations of the Survival Game—Team Games, Individual Games and permutations of both—but the basic idea is this: Armed with a special CO_2 pistol that shoots a harmless marking pellet, a player attempts to take objectives—flags in the woods—and eliminate other players from the Game by shooting them, while avoiding being shot himself.

The Survival Game is, first and foremost, a game, with its roots in humor, honor and fun, not a paramilitary exercise for those who stand slightly to the right of Torquemada. (Such types, in fact, don't like the Survival Game because there is too much frivolity in it; they want something *serious*.) But the Survival Game has a dimension other forms of play lack, a total fantasy environment in which fear, real or imagined, is a stimulating ingredient. Alone in the woods, watching another player sneak toward your position, drawing a bead on his

"Bang, you're dead" has always been our national sport. Until the Game came along, "Bang, you're dead!" was suitable for play only by those under the age of pimples. But no more!

Warning: Do not read this book while playing the Game. You may be distracted and not see that ominous figure lurking behind a log. Then: SPLAT!

stomach with this meaty mass of metal which looks *sooooo* bad but which is a gun only in the semantic sense, worrying if at the same moment someone is drawing a bead on you, then . . . wait, wait, *now!* . . . pulling the trigger, you are stimulated to a degree not found on tennis courts or golf greens. The Survival Game is living Pac-Man, and you are the joystick.

Initially men are attracted to the Survival Game by its physical challenge and head-to-head competition. Women are drawn to it because they rise to the notion that success in the Game hinges on prowess in the previously predominantly male roles of hunter and warrior.

But both men and women soon realize that the Game has so many dimensions that neither strength, hunting experience nor quantity of testosterone assures success. The Game demands a subtle blend of talents in no precise ratio. Guts can compensate for an inability to shoot. Patience can offset woodsmanship. An understanding of game psychology can make up for short legs and a big belly. Anyone can play the Game and no one can play it perfectly.

The step from introduction to obsession is a short one. Because there is such strong visceral pleasure in the Game—the mock fear, the elation, the physical activity—good players and bad players can experience equal thrills. That gut pleasure can be as strong in someone who hides behind a rock for two hours as it is in a player who shoots a half-dozen opponents and captures the flag, for success in the Game is measured in units of fun on the field and nerve tingles in the cranium.

Fun is the name of this Game.

As in any intricate game, the more you know, the more fun the game becomes. And that is where this book comes in. It is designed to put you in the proper spirit for the Survival Game, to teach you enough to give you at least a leg up on your competitors and to pose a few philosophical questions that may expand your appreciation of the Game.

This book is not a handbook for Apocalypse, despite the "survival" in its title. It will not tell you how to find potable water in a subway or how to lay a mine field around your back yard. It will tell you how to have fun in a wonderful, sometimes silly *game,* one that will set your heart pumping, your legs shaking and your ganglia gasping for breath.

Just don't read this book while you are playing the Game, for you may be distracted and not see that ominous figure lurking behind a log. Then:

Splat!

Welcome to the Survival Game.

YOUTH IS A WONDERFUL THING.
WHAT A CRIME TO WASTE IT
ON CHILDREN.
—G. B. Shaw

•

EVERY MAN THINKS MEANLY
OF HIMSELF
FOR NOT HAVING BEEN
A SOLDIER.
—Dr. Johnson

2

THE GAME'S CALLED SURVIVAL

There's a game being played all across this land
That'll test the courage of any good man.
It's based on the drive that keeps us alive.
In the spirit of revival the game's called Survival.
—from the "Survival Game Song"

I'm going to tell you a lot about the Game in this book. I'm going to tell you what it isn't, what it might be, what goes into it and how to play it. I'll give you rules and history and strategy and tips, but first I want to tell you something about singing our song.

The "Survival Game Song" (complete lyrics are in Chapter 18) is harder to sing than the national anthem. Frank Sinatra can't sing it; Barbra Streisand can't sing it. Hardly anyone can sing it because to sing it one must plant one's tongue firmly in one's cheek. And that makes the song come out like this: "Derzzs unh gaum breezn plaudh alh ucrozzh dizsh lundzzs."

The tongue must be in the cheek, you see, because . . . because it's mandatory. Because the Game is a game, and talk of "survival" and "courage" and "drive that keeps us alive" is part of a magnificent illusion into which those who play the Game enter for amusement and stimulation.

The time has come to stop talking and start playing.

That is an important thing to remember when reading this book and when playing the Game, for illusion is what the Game is about—illusion, theater, fun. You can get serious about playing well and winning and even trying to figure out what goes on inside your head when you play, but remember to poke your tongue in your cheek every now and then. That poke will keep the Game in perspective and will keep the Game fun.

Survival 101

You may have seen the Survival Game played on television or read about it in any one of several magazines. If so, you have a general idea of how and where it is played. If not, you now are thoroughly mystified and possibly terrified; no doubt you also are contemplating how to get a refund for the purchase of this book. Before you do, however, stick with me for a moment. I will pose and answer the ten questions most often asked about the Survival Game, which should reassure you. Those of you who know about the Game may wish to jump ahead. Be forewarned, however, there will be a pop quiz on this material somewhere between the covers.

A terrifying sight but only an illusion. The key to the Game is this:
Behind the frightening Nel-Spot pistol, behind the camouflage headnet, the player has his tongue planted firmly in his cheek.

QUESTION NUMBER 1:
"You what?"

We play a grown-up version of Capture the Flag while armed with CO_2 pistols that shoot special marking pellets. The pistols are there so that we can eliminate other players by marking them with the pellets—*splat!*

There are two basic variations. In the Individual Game, players are on their own. Armed with the pistols, wearing protective goggles and often camouflaged, players start the Game from designated positions on the periphery of a playing field. At a signal, players must enter the field and attempt to collect flags from any number of flag stations within the field. Each player carries a compass and map on which the flag stations are indicated. While collecting their flags, players may eliminate other players by shooting them with their CO_2 guns. The first player to collect a flag from each flag station and bring them to a designated base station without being marked by a pellet is the winner.

The Team Game is played on a field with only two flag stations. Players are divided into teams of equal size and each team is assigned a flag. The object of the Team Game is to capture the other team's flag and return it to your flag station while preventing the opposing team from capturing your flag. The first team to do so is the winner. Obviously, during play confrontations between opposing teams occur. That is where the marking gun comes in. When a player is marked by the dye from an opposing player's pellet, he is out of the Game.

Both the Team Game and the Individual Game are played according to strict rules administered by judges on the field. Safety goggles must be worn. Safe handling of the CO_2 gun, called a Nel-Spot, is stressed. Fair play, good sportsmanship and a sense of humor are mandatory. Complete rules for both Games are found in Chapter 10.

QUESTION NUMBER 2:
"Where in hell . . .?"

Some Games, team or individual, are played by people who own Game kits, which include the marking pistol, goggles, face camouflage grease, a compass and the other ingredients necessary for play. Such players may play the Game where and when they like, on private property they own or lease for the purpose of conducting Games.

Most players, however, play on official Game fields operated by sanctioned Survival Game dealers. These fields are located throughout the country. Game dealers rent the necessary equipment to players. The charge for using the field and renting the equipment for a Game is usually about $15. For the name of the Game dealer nearest to you, see Chapter 17.

QUESTION NUMBER 3:
"But why?"

Because it brings out the child in us. Because it is a game pervaded by good humor, honor and sharp competition. Because every Game is different. Because, although many people may play the Game well, no one plays it perfectly. Because the Game crosses social and economic boundaries, permitting doctors and lawyers and factory workers and even writers to have fun together in an endeavor that calls on primitive instincts as well as sophisticated techniques. Because the Game rolls up the sleeves on players' nerve and gives them such a workout that senses are heightened and troubles are forgotten. Because it is fun.

QUESTION NUMBER 4:
"Where is it going?"

Across the country. To colleges, small towns, large towns and cities. To regional, then national competitions to determine the best Survival Game team and the best Individual Game player in the country. Then on to international competition.

QUESTION NUMBER 5:
"Who in their right mind would . . . ?"

Anyone and everyone.

QUESTION NUMBER 6:
"Isn't it sick?"

Not if you keep your tongue in your cheek.

QUESTION NUMBER 7:
"Who are you to tell me how to play?"

How embarrassing that you should ask. In the LASG ratings, I am the number-one player in both Individual and Team Game categories. I played in the first Survival Game, so I have as much experience as anyone. I am also the only writer who didn't have anything to do when the idea of this book came up.

QUESTION NUMBER 8:
"What does LASG stand for?"

Lionel Atwill Survival Game.

Why? Because the Game is fun, pervaded with good humor, honor, and camaraderie.

QUESTION NUMBER 9:

"Isn't this all rather silly?"

The Game, although less than two years old, is rooted in a most eminent tradition, with its own literary *(The Most Dangerous Game)* and cinematic (*Westworld,* a 1973 film directed by Michael Crichton and starring Yul Brynner and Richard Benjamin) heritage. Silly, you bombastic booby, what could be silly about running around the woods shooting at people with paint pellets while screaming dialogue from a comic book—*Powee, aughrrgh, splat. Of course it's silly!*

QUESTION NUMBER 10:

"Where can I learn more about the National Survival Game?"

Right here. Turn the page.

3

THE ROOTS OF THE GAME

This quotation by Menander, the Greek comedic dramatist, was appended to the letter inviting people to play in the first Survival Game. The Game's founders, Charles Gaines, Hayes Noel and Bob Gurnsey, suggested players ponder that thought as they determined their strategies.

Discounting quirks of fate—gargoyles that fall from buildings to flatten people in the streets and such—Menander's observation rings true to me. Sort of "You are what you eat" on a cosmic level. I think it holds, too, for the creations of men: Our dispositions mold what we make or conceive or do.

Now you may view that notion as a cosmic crock. But if you find even a glint of truth in it, you will agree that the dispositions of the men who conceived the Game have bearing on what the Game is about, and their initial concept should influence how the rest of us play the Game today. Listen, then, to the saga of the Survival Game.

Sketches first:

Charles Gaines is 41 years old. He is a writer—novels, nonfiction and screenplays. His books include the novel *Stay Hungry* and a nonfiction work, *Pumping Iron,* both of which are about body building. Together those books brought flexing out of the closet and Arnold Schwarzenegger into our living rooms. Charles lives in New Hampshire with his wife and three children.

Hayes Noel, 43, is a New York stock and options trader, one of those guys in odd-colored coats who mill about the floor of the Stock Exchange shouting in tongues. Hayes is very successful at his job. He is a serious runner, a former college football player and an old friend of Charles. He is married and has a three-year-old daughter.

Bob Gurnsey is pushing 41. He, too, lives in New Hampshire, ten miles from Charles. He is married and has two children. Bob now is the full-time director of the National Survival Game, Inc. Before that, he owned a ski shop. Before that, he was a deep-water sailor and a sports-car racer.

I purposely have skimped on details about these three men. This is not *People* magazine, and their private lives are their private lives. I will tell you of some traits they share, however—those common qualities of disposition that shaped this Game.

All three are competitors; all three enjoy competition for its own sake. Together, at a dull party, they have been known to bet on the length of a dog or the number of bricks in a fireplace. Their love of competition exists in a spirit of childlike fun. They enjoy their competition, and, believe me, others enjoy being around them when they are competing, because that spirit of fun pervades. I cannot say the same about a lot of country-club tennis players I know.

Second, Gaines, Noel and Gurnsey enjoy camaraderie. They like to be with friends, male and female, and they relish the humor and honor that accompany friendship.

Third, all three are men of action. They revel in risk and the need for decisiveness that risk demands. Option trading is risky. Writing is risky. Lordy be, working for a company that is founded on a gun that shoots paint pellets is risky. That enchantment with action has pervaded their lives. Gurnsey raced cars. Charles has scuba dived in the open ocean in the company of a hooked marlin. Hayes once was set upon by thugs in New York. He responded by shrieking obscenities and damn near beating one to death with a convenient garbage can.

It would be all too simple to classify these three as macho beer guys, living life to the fullest, going for the gusto and hating quiche. They live life fully, yes, but macho they are not. There is no braggadocio among them, and they share traits of warmth and tenderness—softness, perhaps, although that word may imply (to the macho mind) weakness, and weak they are not.

The characters now are in position. Let's see how the Game evolved.

It started in 1976 with a cape buffalo, one of those big, mean things with horns that roam Africa. A friend of Hayes's had returned from a safari on which he had hunted a buff. He had told Hayes of the excitement, of the surge of adrenaline and of the heightened sense of perception that came from the danger of facing that animal. He swore he could smell and hear and taste and feel more clearly in that environment of fear. It was a sensory high, a drugless high.

Hayes and his friend were walking through the woods when Hayes heard the story. Hayes suggested that, as a lark, they try to recreate some of that feeling, that on their way back to the house they stalk one another as a hunter stalks his game. As they did so, Hayes recognized

Gaines, Gurnsey, Noel.
Photo by David Seybold

something of what his friend had told him. A tingle. A feeling of being particularly well tuned and alive.

Later in the year, on the sand of Jupiter Beach, Florida, where they were vacationing, Hayes told the story to Charles. Charles agreed that in an atmosphere of danger, one's senses are enhanced. The problem, they agreed, was creating the illusion of a dangerous atmosphere, for few people would risk true danger for a sensory reward. Then they started talking about Hayes's mock stalk, and their dispositions began to shape the conversation. Gaines argued that in such a situation, a country boy could outsmart a city boy, because a country boy knows how to hunt, knows the woods, knows, in short, how to survive.

Not so, argued Hayes. The skills to survive on Wall Street or in the subway could be transmuted successfully to the African veld or the New Hampshire woods. Suddenly, an intellectual discussion of sensory awareness metamorphosed into a debate—a challenge.

Competition.

Fun.

The argument did not die on that Florida beach. It fermented over the next few years, resurfacing from time to time: in New Hampshire (where Gurnsey joined in), in New York and finally in a duck blind one Thanksgiving on the Maine coast. In that blind was Ritchie White, a friend from New Hampshire, a registered forester and an ardent hunter who took his woodsmanship seriously. The ducks were flying fast and furious but nowhere fast enough to match the pace of the discussion. "Hayes," Ritchie finally said, "you could be anywhere in those woods," he pointed to the thick Maine forest behind them, "and I could sneak up on you and cut your throat."

The gauntlet now was thrown. Only the weapon had to be chosen. It was found in a forestry-supply catalog by a friend of Charles' a short while later: the Nel-Spot 007 Color Marking Gun, "a real help in game population census. . . . Mark trees in swamps or difficult mountainous terrain. . . . [Telephone] poles and other objects can now be marked from a distance. A real time saver."

And an implement for determining who could survive.

Gaines and Noel ordered Nel-Spots. They found out the gun was accurate; they found out, by shooting Charles's son, Shelby, in the rear end, that the pellet did not hurt much (Hayes insists he volunteered his rump and Charles insists he offered his, but Shelby says, and I believe him, that Hayes and Charles were chicken). Charles, Hayes and Gurnsey then got together and formulated the rules of the Individual Survival Game.

Invitations went out in the spring of 1981. Nine people immediately replied, returning checks for $175 to cover the cost of Nel-Spots, goggles and ample food and booze. All of the respondents were friends, some from the city, some from the country, so it appeared that the city mouse–country mouse argument would be settled once and for all.

On a sunny June day in 1981, we arrived at Charles's house in New Hampshire: Bob Jones, 47, a novelist, staff writer for *Sports Illustrated* and an experienced hunter; Ronnie Simpkins, 32, a farmer from Alabama and a master turkey hunter; Jerome Gary, 35, a New York film producer; Carl Sandquist, 38, a New Hampshire contracting estimator; Ritchie White, 37, the New Hampshire forester who had told Hayes he could cut his neck in the woods; Ken Barrett, 32, a New York venture capitalist with much hunting experience; Joe Drinon, 37, a stockbroker from New Hampshire and a former Golden Gloves boxer; Bob Carlson, 40, a trauma surgeon from Alabama and a hunter; and myself, 35, a writer for *Sports Afield,* a hunter and a Vietnam vet, who had had the unpleasurable experience of leading reconnaissance missions in Vietnam in 1968, a decidedly poor year. Plus, of course, the committee: Charles, Hayes and Bob.

No one knew what to expect. We fondled the pistols and painted a few of Charles's trees and, by tape and pencil, recorded our strategies for posterity. We sized each other up and tried to psych each other out, too: "I hear you got a deer with a muzzle loader last year," I overheard Bob Carlson say to Ken Barrett.

"Yeah," answered Barrett. "Nice six-point buck. Do you hunt?"

"Little bit," answered Carlson, "but I had a poor year last year. Only got six deer."

The night before the Game the committee held a Calcutta raffle. One by one, in the order in which we were seeded, we went on the block. There were a lot of giggles as the city boys were sold for less than the price of a case of beer. Everyone thought their chances of winning were slim. Then the hunters went up. Jones went for good money; so did Simpkins and White and Barrett. Finally, the number-one seed came up for auction: me.

Graciously Hayes slapped down $140 for me. "LRRP's gonna win; LRRP's gonna win," he shouted out. LRRP is an acronym for Long Range Reconnaissance Patrols, which in Vietnam were three- to five-man units that did some messy work; I had the misfortune of having served in one for a while. Also, I had attended a bunch of Army schools—Airborne, Ranger, Special Forces—which theoretically gave me a leg up on may fellow Game players. That I would disprove the next day.

Like many a Super Bowl, the first Survival Game, seen as a whole, was less exciting than the prelude. Rather than give a play-by-play, which even Howard Cosell could not enliven, I will recount the highlights.

Ken Barrett was the first to dye. Within ten minutes, he ambushed and shot Gary, but his pellet did not burst. As Ken reloaded, Gary walked up calm as could be, stuck his pistol in Ken's neck and asked, "Give up?" Ken is no fool; five minutes later he was popping a beer.

Gurnsey's fate was less noble. Simpkins, the Alabama turkey hunter, got the drop on him and with a syrupy "Now hold it raht tha-uh" forced Gurnsey to drop his gun. Then, in a dash, Simpkins was on Gurnsey, wiping his hand across Gurns's belly. Gurnsey looked down; a splotch of red paint crossed his gut like an unruly appendectomy scar. Simpkins smiled. He had run out of CO_2, but, like his rebel ancestors, refused to acknowledge defeat. So he took out Gurnsey with a bluff and a paint pellet in his hand. Simpkins was the only player in that first game to count coup.

Bob Carlson abandoned his strategy early in the Game in favor of simply shooting people. In all, he took out five players. "Wonderful," I heard him say after play, "this really relieves your tensions. Takes away all aggression. Very therapeutic." Dr. Robert Carlson, trauma surgeon, gave the Survival Game its first identifiable role model: the Death Doctor.

Gaines, the country-boy-is-a-survivor advocate, survived several shootouts, and once had the drop on Simpkins. But Simpkins dove over a log, executed a near-perfect forward roll and came up running. Gaines just stood there with his unfired gun in hand. Something in him kept him from splattering Simpkins at close range when he had the chance. "I guess I'm a little softer than I like to think," he later said.

Hayes never got the chance to do anyone in, but he proved he could run like hell and that a city kid can survive—almost. He had three flags in his belt and was going for the fourth when the Death Doctor did him in.

And me? Hell, I was a disaster. I shot it up with Hayes early on, but that was inconclusive. Next, I came up on Gaines. We shot back and forth, then I hurled a moldy onion I had found in the woods and yelled, "Grenade." My reputation helped, I think, because the onion grenade took Gaines off guard. He fired wildly, I charged, and at ten yards I shot him in the leg. But the pellet did not break. He leveled his gun and ordered me to surrender. I pulled a Simpkins roll, but with less success: My glasses and goggles came off, and I was blind. Charles chased me around a bush a couple of times before smacking me in the leg. What kind of guy would shoot a blind man, I ask?

The winner of that first game was Ritchie White, the New Hampshire forester. No one ever saw Ritchie, and he never fired a shot. He crept through the woods from station to station, gathering flags as easily as a schoolgirl gathers flowers.

The play was less than spectacular compared to some Games I've seen since, but there was a spirit to that first Game that will be hard to capture again. The weekend bubbled with humor, honor, fun and obnoxiously friendly, yet intense competition. Those feelings, I believe, reflected the dispositions of the founders of the Game.

What has happened to the Game since then is, as they say, history. I wrote a story about the Game for *Sports Afield*. Bob Jones wrote a story about the Game for *Sports Illustrated*. Tim Cahill, who attended as a spectator, wrote a story about the Game for *Outside*. Then newspapers and television picked it up, The National Survival Game, Inc. was formed, and here we are.

And where are we?

Why, playing *a game* rooted in a tradition of honor, humor, competition and fun.

4

MEET THE PLAYERS

The temptation is great to categorize those who play the Game. A critic sees a player who drives a truck and collects guns, and immediately in his mind all Game players are blue-collar workers with fascist leanings. A proponent of the Game who knows a Game-playing lawyer is tempted to pronounce that the Game attracts none but professionals.

Both categorizations are unfair. In fact, all categorizations are unfair from what I can see. I have tried my best to come up with a category as broad as possible to hold all Survival Game players, but at each attempt I soon think of an exception.

I think that speaks well for the Game. The game is eminently egalitarian and is relatively inexpensive, certainly cheaper per person per hour than tennis or golf. It does not necessitate clothing or gear that might reflect social or economic background. To the contrary, the uniform of the Game—camouflage—disguises every vestige of status, right down to covering up a patrician nose. And it does not demand any special skills. The Game is for everyone and anyone: men and women, athletes and klutzes, doctors and truck drivers, Democrats and Republicans, blacks and whites and yellows and browns, straights and gays, liberals and conservatives, rich and poor, old and young. The only group not permitted to play are people who can't put their tongues in their cheeks every now and then.

Those Who Dared

Let's look at a few people who play the Game. I selected these players not so much for what they do in real life—although that had some bearing—but for the ways in which they perceive the Game. Besides vital statistics, I asked them but one question: Why do you play the Survival Game? I have edited their comments only to clarify, to eliminate foul, abusive language that might offend some, and to put words in their mouths when they couldn't think of anything to say. The thumbnail sketch of each player is compiled from their vital statistics and from my own prejudiced views. Herewith are Those Who Dared (to play the Game and talk to me):

Patricia Gaines

Patricia is 37, the mother of three children, a successful artist and book author and the wife of Charles Gaines, one of the guiding spirits of the Survival Game. She is a devastatingly beautiful, delicate lady, who, because she has had to listen to nonstop Game talk for the last three or four years, should despise the very mention of the Survival Game. However, she does not.

"In the beginning I was not that enthusiastic about it. I didn't quite understand it, and I thought it a little macho. I also felt terribly left out. There did not seem to be any role for me in the action except that of sandwich maker.

"Then I saw the first Game. It seemed to be authentically good for everybody. So therapeutic, so full of bonding and joy. It was virtually impossible from that point on to have a negative thought or feel bad about the Game. I did a complete about-face.

"I first played to see what all the excitement was about from the participant's point of view. But I also had personal reasons. Traditionally, little girls are denied that sense of play, fun, competition and sport. I felt that was rather crippling. I was to always sit on the sidelines, play with my dolls and not get dirty, which is what I did. So I decided to play the Game for me.

"I couldn't believe how terrified I was. For the first time I could understand a little about the psychology of a soldier, a very young soldier. A couple of times I wanted to turn tail and run, or I wanted to hide, or once I wanted to banzai down the hill and let people shoot me to get it over with.

"I realized, then, how important it is to put myself into situations I would not ordinarily participate in, because it is a chance to grow. Too, I don't think women often have this type of opportunity—a really heightened, condensed, distilled encounter where you are unified in purpose. All your feelings and perceptions are heightened, and the sense of bonding is immense.

"The psychology of the Game has always interested me, because I think that people reveal a lot about themselves in the way they play. I was angered by my own passivity. I could have shot players a couple of times, and I let them go by.

"But mainly I play because it is such a good game."

Shane Lautenslager

Shane is 28, married and lives in Livermore, California, near San Jose—to which he knows the way. He works for Verbatim, a Silicone Valley manufacturer of floppy discs for computers (this book was written on a Verbatim floppy disc, which has absolutely nothing to do with the Survival Game, but I thought Shane might just like to know). Shane plays the Game at least once a month and is credited with creating the first computer-generated declaration of war, challenging another Silicone Valley firm, for which Shane's brother works, to a Survival Game.

"I play because it's fun. I do not like guns; I am not interested in warfare. But this is fun—comic-book fun. You get to go out and challenge yourself against someone else who is trying to do the same thing.

"I probably would not play if a whole lot of macho types were going out there. We go out to let off a bunch of steam we have built up all week—all month. For the guys I play with, the biggest part of the Game is honor, and everybody is honorable whom I have seen.

"The business I'm in is very high pressured and I'm usually indoors. When I go to work, I see the sun come up; when I go home, I see the sun go down. The rest of the day I am almost locked indoors and under pressure all the time. The Game gets me outside and relieves that pressure. And it is great fun."

Ken Barrett

Until a few months ago Ken, 34, lived with his family in Westchester County, New York, and worked as a venture capitalist in Manhattan. Recently, Ken ventured away from venture capitalizing and capitalized on a capital idea of the folks at the Survival Game, to wit, that they venture forward and get someone else to help in the business. Ken is now that someone, which is capital. That he should abandon his former line of work and join up with the Survival Game speaks well for the Game and its future. There is an outside chance that Ken may have joined so that he can play more and improve his record of past performances. In the first Game Ken was the first man out, and in his starring role in an ABC documentary of the Game Ken suffered the ignominious fate of being shot within the first 10 seconds of play—by me, of all people.

"I see the Game as great fun, allowing adults to play as they did in childhood. However, as the Game progresses, a real shot of adrenaline makes the play very real and exciting—and that makes you feel very alive.

The Game is better than any hockey, tennis or organized ball game I've ever played. You run on 12 cylinders all the time, and we rarely get a chance to do that in grown-up living."

Mary Conlin

Mary is a nurse, 35 years old, and the mother of two teen-age children. She lives on Merritt Island, Florida, just north of Cocoa Beach and south of the Kennedy Space Center. Mary was interviewed on television about her participation in the Game by Phil Donahue, a formidable interviewer. Mary not only stood up admirably to Donahue but won over his audience.

"I play because it's fun; it's unfortunate that we have to explain why we enjoy ourselves.

"I work on the surgical side of a hospital. There is a lot of death and dying there that I see every day. Going out into the woods to play the Game is a catharsis of all that."

Michael and Sarah Foley

Mike, 30, and Sarah, 26, live and work in New York City, Mike as a consulting computer analyst, Sarah as a sales and marketing manager for a British publication. The Foleys, obviously, are married, and, not obviously, are British. They play the Survival Game in Cambridge, New York, which is four-and-a-half hours from the city by car. The Foleys have played in some seven Games.

Sarah: "I play for fun. It is exciting and stimulating. It gives me some much needed exercise that I don't normally get. And it brings back some of the rather childish memories of hide-and-seek.

"It is particularly enjoyable that Mike and I can do something together that we both enjoy, and we have no qualms about being on opposite teams. Playing together is important. We have very different interests otherwise, which we pursue in our own directions, but this is one thing we can do together.

"I haven't found anybody who thinks I'm sick. Childish, perhaps, but not weird. We're really keen on the Game, and we want to get better and better at it. I need a lot of target practice."

Mike: "I more or less echo my wife's sentiments. We're probably not the right couple to talk to. Our reasons are not very spectacular.

"I was a little surprised when I first played. I expected to feel scared or something like that. Instead, all I felt was fun. I found myself giggling.

"I'm not altogether happy about shooting Sarah. I'd rather she were on

Game player: Mary Conlin, mother of two, surgical nurse. "I play because it's fun; it's unfortunate that we have to explain why we enjoy ourselves."

Game player: Michael Foley, thirty, computer analyst. "I probably would think twice about shooting my wife, Sara. On the other hand, she hasn't crossed my sights as yet."

Game player: Sarah Foley, twenty-six, New Yorker, a sales and marketing manager for a British publication. "I need a lot of target practice."

my team, although I think she's rather dying to get a crack shot at me. But I'd probably think twice about firing on her. On the other hand, she hasn't crossed my sights as yet."

I could write up interviews with a dozen or more Game players, but I found that the people I talked with are frightfully normal and their reasons for playing rather straightforward and mundane: fun, camaraderie, competition and the like. So rather than bore you with more happy people spouting sane comments, I will conclude this chapter with an interview with myself.

Lionel Atwill

Tony (from middle name Anthony) is 37. A contributing editor to *Sports Afield* magazine and a freelancer for other publications, he lives with his wife Elena and four-year-old daughter Amanda in southern Vermont. From his number-one seeding in the first Survival Game, a status bestowed because of his army service in Vietnam, Atwill's ranking has fallen each time he has played since then.

"When I first learned of the Game—that first Game—I adjusted the veteran's chip on my shoulder and thought that the whole idea was nothing more than a way for all the guys who were getting their fourth graduate degree while I was fighting a war to show that they could cut the mustard too.

"Since playing the Game a half dozen times and since writing this book, I have changed that view. I've shed my veteran's chip and now I see the Game as a fine kids' game—for grown-up kids. I play because I enjoy the company of the people with whom I play and the absolute silliness of the Game itself. I do not take the Game seriously, yet no one cares that I don't take it seriously. Hard to say that even about weekend tennis or golf."

Secondhand Comments from Game Players Around the Country

G. Patton, Slapakid, Iowa: "No bastard ever won a Game by dying for his team. You win a Game by making the other poor bastard dye for his."

A. Caesar, Rome, New York: *"Veni, vedi, painti."*

D. MacArthur, Manilla, Indiana: "I shall repaint."

N. Bonaparte, Paris, Maine: "The pellet that will paint me is not yet cast."

COMPONENTS OF THE GAME

5

GUNS AND PELLETS

Like the gun of the ditty, which does not refer to the Nel-Spot but to a piece of anatomy (if in doubt, ask an ex-serviceman), the gun of the Game is for fun. Designed to mark cows, telephone poles and trees, the Nel-Spot 007 has found its place in the sun splattering people in the Survival Game.

The Nel-Spot is but a tool, a sophisticated, long-range paintbrush. But because it looks so ominous, because of its James Bondian nomenclature, because it is called *a gun* (and it is a gun only in the semantic sense), the Nel-Spot adds a lot of metaphorical baggage to the Survival Game. And important baggage it is.

"Whoa baby, don't point that paintbrush (water-filled balloon, squirt gun, or rotten tomato) at me!"

See, it wouldn't work. That the gun looks like *a gun* adds great weight to the Game. The gun is a tool that mimics a weapon. In its mimicry it becomes symbolic, and that symbolism, with its element of real or imagined fear, heightens the fantasy of the Game. The gun makes the Game work on several levels. So to play well, best you should learn all you can about the Nel-Spot 007.

Designed to mark cows, telephone poles, and trees, the Nel-Spot 007
has found its place splattering people.

Aunt Nellie

If you like to talk cc's, decibels, and bytes, then you will want to know the Nel-Spot's specs:

NEL-SPOT 007

Caliber: .68
Action: bolt
Magazine: tubular, gravity feed, 14
   pellets
Weight: 2 lbs. 3 ozs.

Length: 11 inches
Sights: fixed, open notch
Trigger Pull: 5 lbs.
Safety: cross block
Power: 12-gram CO_2, 750 psi
Range: 30 yards

If you don't care about such stuff, then at least learn the basic nomenclature—trigger, bolt, rear sight, front sight, magazine cap, loading port, grip—by referring to the diagram. You will need to know these things to operate the gun safely.

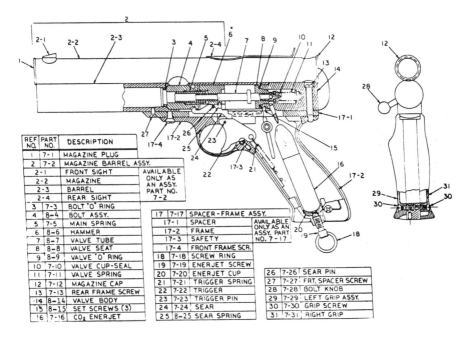

REF NO.	PART NO.	DESCRIPTION
1	7-1	MAGAZINE PLUG
2	7-2	MAGAZINE BARREL ASSY.
2-1		FRONT SIGHT
2-2		MAGAZINE
2-3		BARREL
2-4		REAR SIGHT
3	7-3	BOLT "O" RING
4	8-4	BOLT ASSY.
5	7-5	MAIN SPRING
6	8-6	HAMMER
7	8-7	VALVE TUBE
8	8-8	VALVE SEAT
9	8-9	VALVE "O" RING
10	7-10	VALVE CUP-SEAL
11	7-11	VALVE SPRING
12	7-12	MAGAZINE CAP
13	7-13	REAR FRAME SCREW
14	8-14	VALVE BODY
15	8-15	SET SCREWS (3)
16	7-16	CO_2 ENERJET

(2-1, 2-2, 2-3, 2-4 AVAILABLE ONLY AS AN ASSY. PART NO. 7-2)

REF NO.	PART NO.	DESCRIPTION
17	7-17	SPACER-FRAME ASSY.
17-1		SPACER
17-2		FRAME
17-3		SAFETY
17-4		FRONT FRAME SCR.
18	7-18	SCREW RING
19	7-19	ENERJET SCREW
20	7-20	ENERJET CUP
21	7-21	TRIGGER SPRING
22	7-22	TRIGGER
23	7-23	TRIGGER PIN
24	7-24	SEAR
25	8-25	SEAR SPRING

(17-1, 17-2, 17-3 AVAILABLE ONLY AS AN ASSY. PART NO. 7-17)

REF NO.	PART NO.	DESCRIPTION
26	7-26	SEAR PIN
27	7-27	FRT. SPACER SCREW
28	7-28	BOLT KNOB
29	7-29	LEFT GRIP ASSY.
30	7-30	GRIP SCREW
31	7-31	RIGHT GRIP

Reprinted with the permission of the Nelso Paint Company.

Although the Nel-Spot shoots relatively harmless marking pellets, it can hurt, possibly damage and certainly annoy if not handled properly. Two simple rules will forestall much embarrassment and possible harm:

1. Do not point the gun at anyone or anything you do not intend to shoot.
2. Keep the safety on when you are not contemplating shooting someone.

I have noticed at many Games that players unaccustomed to firearms are casual with the Nel-Spot, wheeling it by spectators who are not goggled, even firing it into the ground (to the chagrin of well-dressed nonplayers splattered in the process). Suffice it to say that even though the gun is not a dangerous firearm, treat it as such. If you wish to practice your marksmanship prior to play, do so from behind a designated firing line and shoot at a designated target. Please don't splatter every tree, bush, car and dog in sight! Be particularly careful around spectators.

Think. Be careful.

Loading

Before doing anything with the Nel-Spot, find the safety, the button aft of the trigger, and put it on. When pushed *from left to right,* the safety will block the pull of the trigger and render the gun safe. When pushed *from right to left,* normally with the trigger finger (on a right-handed shooter), the gun will fire.

To find out what the safety is doing, look at the button. If a red band is visible around the button (on the left side of the trigger guard), the safety is *off.* Red means danger; the gun will fire. If the red band is not visible, the gun is safe.

With the safety on, remove the left grip cap by pulling out on the indentation at the bottom of the grip. Now turn the screw ring at the bottom of the grip counterclockwise. Note that this backs off a small cup within the grip.

Keep turning until you can insert a 12-gram CO_2 cartridge into the cartridge cradle in the grip frame. The rounded bottom of the cartridge should nestle in the cup attached to the screw ring. The pointed top of the cartridge should align with the puncture pin at the top of the grip frame.

Now turn the screw ring clockwise until the pointed top of the CO_2 contacts the puncture pin. Make sure that the pin is centered on the top of the cartridge.

Replace the grip cap. It is important to do this now, for if things foul up when you puncture the CO_2 and the grip cap is off, the gas will escape into

The bottom of the CO_2 cartridge should nestle in the cup attached to the ring screw. The top of the cartridge should align with the puncture pin.

With the grip cap in place, hold the gun to your ear like a good safe-cracker. Turn the ring slowly until you hear a satisfying HISSSS.

Load 14 pellets in the magazine. If you are using a Survival Game reloading magazine (pictured), you can jam the tube into the magazine as an extender.

your face or onto your hand. CO_2 is extremely cold, and the grip cap will protect you from frostbite.

With the cap in place, hold the gun to your ear like a good safecracker. Turn the screw ring—*slowly*—until you hear a satisfying *hisss*. That is gas entering the gun.

Now turn the ring one quarter-turn more to ensure a good seal.

If you feel and hear a mad rush of cold gas, you have cranked too much. Carefully remove the CO_2 cartridge and insert a new one.

Check again: Is the safety on? Good, now remove the magazine cap. Load 14 pellets and replace the cap. If you are using a Survival Game reloading tube (see Chapter 9), you can jam the tube into the gun's magazine and leave it there.

Cocking

Grip the pistol firmly with your right hand and grab the bolt handle with your left. Lift the bolt handle up until it clears the notch in the barrel and stops. Pull back firmly. With a CO_2 cartridge properly seated in the gun, the bolt will lock back. *It will not lock without a cartridge or with an empty cartridge.*

Lift the bolt handle until it clears the notch in the barrel; then pull back. The bolt will not stay back unless the gun is charged with a full CO_2 cartridge.

With the bolt back, tilt the gun until a pellet drops from the magazine through the loading port and into the chamber. You can watch all of this going on. If your gun is not fully loaded, you may have to roll the pellets around to get one to drop through the loading port.

Push the bolt forward and down, locking the handle into the notch. Be careful not to pinch a wayward second pellet trying to roll into the loading port. The gun now is ready to fire.

If you are left-handed, operating the safety and cocking the gun will be difficult. But so are scissors. Sorry, that is the curse of the sinister set.

Firing

Before you pull the trigger, you should know how to aim the gun and how to hold it. The front sight is little more than a metal blip (called a blade sight in gun talk). The rear sight is a rectangular piece of metal with a notch in the middle (an open sight). Neither sight on the Nel-Spot is adjustable, although some fooling with a hammer and a file can change the point of impact (see Chapter 9).

To aim the gun, align the front blip in the middle of the rear notch. The top of the front sight should be level with the top of the rear sight. Now place the target—say the chest of your boss, who is playing on the opposing team—on top of the front sight. What you see should look like this:

Notice that you are looking at objects on three planes: the rear sight, front sight, and target. That is a problem for most of us. The accepted solution is to focus on the front sight and let the rear sight and target blur. However, since the sights of the Nel-Spot are so coarse and the accuracy of the gun so unreliable (compared to a real pistol), I prefer not to bother with proper pistol-shooting form. Instead, I focus on the target. That way, I can see what the guy is doing and shoot fast, run, hide or surrender, as I see fit.

There is another way to aim that lends itself to quick shooting, particularly at moving targets. It is called *instinctive shooting* and is predicated on one's ability to point quickly and accurately where the eyes look.

It works. Look at something on the wall. Now bring up your finger and point at it. See. If you had a front and rear sight on your finger, you would not be any more accurate.

Consider the Nel-Spot as an extension of your hand, a sixth finger. Look at a target, point that sixth finger at it and fire without hesitating. Concentrate on the target, not the gun. Forget the sights. Follow through by not dropping your hands. Keep pointing after you have fired. With practice, it will work.

How you hold the Nel-Spot has more effect on what you hit than how you sight the gun. The key to hitting anything is steadiness, meaning support. So rest the gun over a rock or log or clump of dirt where and when you can.

The more hands you can get on the gun, the better. Although it worked well for John Wayne, Hoppy and Aaron Burr, the classic extended-arm dueling position is passé. The Hill Street Blues combat crouch is in.

If you are right-handed, grasp the grip with your right hand. Now place the heel of your hand and the butt of the gun in your open left palm. Do not lock your arms. Square your shoulders to the target. Crouch. Let the gun and your hands float. And when the sights drop in on the target: *Splat!*

An alternative position, effective when sitting or standing in the woods, is to grab a small tree with the left hand (assuming the shooter is right-handed) and lay the barrel of the gun or the right wrist across the left forearm.

Naturally, the most satisfying shooting position is from the hip. Cock Nellie, scream, splatter a tree, cock again, run, dive behind a log, threaten, curse, shoot again . . . on and on. May not hit anything, but damn, it's fun.

Shooting the gun is simplicity itself: pull the trigger. If you want to be suave, take a deep breath, exhale slowly, hold your breath when your lungs are half full, then ever so slowly *squeeze* off a shot. Probably you will be shot long before you get to the squeezing part, but some people just have to do everything by the book.

Cradle the butt of the gun and the shooting hand in the palm of the opposite hand. The magazine extender pictured is a cigar tube.

The Gun in the Game

The holster is handy for carrying the gun after the Game, when you are standing around sucking on a beer and swapping lies. But it serves little purpose in play. Best to carry the gun at the ready in your hand, which means with the muzzle up to prevent a chambered pellet from sliding forward in the barrel (and sometimes right on out the barrel, if you are running hard). The safety should be on. The only time you should keep the safety off, in fact, is when you are lying in ambush for someone. Then, the small metallic click of the safety sliding off might give away your position. Best to let an opponent learn of your position by hearing the splat of a marking pellet on his chest.

Where to Shoot

Aim for the middle of the body, which means from the shoulder to the hip. That is the biggest target. Also, no one likes to be hit in the head; it doesn't hurt that much, but it is scary.

Err on the low side and in front of the target. That means it is better to shoot low on someone than high. Low gives you the legs and the possibility of hitting brush or dirt in front of your victim, which can throw up a shower of marking paint. A shot in front of your intended victim when he or she is running may hit a branch, leaving a mist of marking paint in the air through which the poor sap may pass. Also, one inevitably shoots behind on running targets.

Nel-Spot Maintenance

An occasional drop of household oil on working parts will keep your gun in good order. Squirt everything visible through the bolt slot. Squirt the trigger sear mechanism, accessible with the left grip removed.

If a marking pellet ruptures in the gun, don't worry. Clean out the gunk with a rag wrapped around the end of a dowel. For more sophisticated maintenance, which is rarely needed, see Chapter 9.

Pellets

The marking pellets used in the Game today are a great improvement over the old pellets. They are stable, they rupture easily, they fly accurately and the marking gel is water soluble.

If, after a Game, you have pellets left over, store them in a dry location. Should you detect any separation in the marking gel, put the pellets in a tube, clamp your thumb over the top and give everything a shake for three or four minutes; that will put the marking gel back into suspension.

If you should inherit a tube or two of old pellets, keep them in a very dry area. If the pellets absorb moisture, they can be dried out by placing them in a very low oven (150 degrees) for ten minutes. The marking fluid in the old pellets separates easily, causing the pellets to shoot erratically. To thoroughly mix the fluid, remove two pellets from a full tube, clamp your thumb on the top and shake like mad for five minutes or longer.

Do not allow any pellets, new or old, to freeze, and never shoot a frozen pellet.

The marking gel from the new pellets can be removed with water. The old marking fluid can be removed with mineral spirits, if you catch the splat before the paint sets. Otherwise, sorry about that.

Should some marking gel get through your goggles and into your eyes, flush thoroughly with water and consult a physician.

Never eat a pellet, and keep pellets, the gun and CO_2 cartridges out of the hands of children.

Now go play with your gun.

6

CLOTHING AND CAMOUFLAGE

One wonderful thing about the Game is that you do not need to wear a multilaminated wondersuit or a shirt emblazoned with a caricature of a reptile in order to play. Jeans work. Overalls work. Almost any old clothes work and work well.

There is, however, a type of clothing that enhances the Game: *camouflage*. Camo hides you in the woods (and you will want to hide some time) and camo heightens the fantasy.

Believe me, it does. Pac-Man would not be the real thing if he were a grape with gums. By the same token, a Game player is just a guy running around the woods, unless he is wearing camouflage. Camo garbs you in a different frame of mind.

Picture it: Milford Puckermeyer, gentle but certified public accountant, slips off his Weejuns, his button-down shirt, his three-piece polyester suit and slides into camo. *Zap!* He becomes Milford the Magnificent, scourge of the woods.

It's as easy as that.

You do not need a $150 camo jumpsuit with 57 pockets and a secret compartment for cyanide pills. You need the cheapest camo you can find. I advise that for two reasons. First, you are going to be splattered—sometime, somewhere—and although the new Game marking pellets are water soluble, there is a fine chance that after play you will sit around sipping beer and the dye will set. Now a lavender splotch on the crotch is a fine battle scar but an ill-suited adornment for a costly camo suit. Second, you will be leaping, crawling and scrambling through an assortment of puckerbrush. Your camo will self-destruct within a year's play. So look for cheap camo.

Where? Try Army–Navy stores. Sometimes they carry surplus camo fatigues. Next, try sporting-goods stores. Finally, pick up one of the fantasy fighting magazines such as *Soldier of Fortune*. There you will find ads for mail-order firms selling camouflaged everything.

Patterns? It doesn't really matter. Pick something you like, something that goes well with your favorite tie.

Colors? Try to match seasonal vegetation: green for spring and summer; tan for fall. It is bad taste to mix colors. For evening Games, basic black is the only choice.

No camouflage.

Donning camouflage.

Good camouflage.

Perfect camouflage.

Accessories

Wear combat boots if they accentuate the fantasy for you. Otherwise, sneakers or running shoes are fine. If you are hard core, you will spray-paint them olive drab.

Bare hands can give you away. If you don't want to smear grease over your mitts, get a pair of camo cotton gloves.

Headwear is important to break up the telltale oval outline of the head. Almost any camo hat will do. It can be decorated fashionably with leaves and branches. Also suitable is the Game Headnet, particularly when crowned with a camo handkerchief rolled into a sweatband and festooned with leaves and litter.

Optional accessories include camouflaged anything: wallets, shoelaces, underwear, support stockings, earrings or breath spray. One can never be too thin, too rich or too well camouflaged.

Greasing Up

Even if you wear a three-piece camo suit, if you don't do something about your face, you will be seen. The old physiognomy simply has to go.

The simplest solution is to wear a Game Headnet, designed after years of research by our research-and-development staff to hide the most hideous face while permitting full use of eyes, ears and other extraneous senses. The face mask is worn on the head like a sack. It is made of camo netting, which keeps out bugs and permits some air to pass through. An elastic band holds the eyeholes firmly to the eyes.

All in all, the headnet is the most practical means of face disguise; however, it lacks a certain aesthetic appeal. Specifically, it makes you feel as if you are dressed to rob a bank.

The alternative, then, is camo grease, which disguises as well as the headnet while providing yet another wonderful ritual: greasing up! Camo grease is available at just about any sporting goods store or through Survival Game dealers.

There is a fine art to applying camo grease. The Army has spent thousands of dollars, perhaps millions, to come up with the right blending of highlights and shadows, which, when applied to the face, will make anyone vanish.

Surprisingly, this subtle pattern is the same one Clearasil recommends for applying its famous medication to oily skin.

Greasing up is a fine art. Apply camo grease following the directions that come with a tube of Clearasil.

You will need two colors to do an effective job: a light shade and a dark shade. Dark green and light green work well in summer. Brown and tan are fine for fall. Black and almost any other color work well all the time. Apply the dark pigment to the shiny areas of your face (forehead, cheekbones, nose and chin). Apply the lighter shade everywhere else (around the eyes, under the nose, and under the chin). See, just like a visit to the Elizabeth Arden counter.

Of course, if you want to wing it and paint up your face like a Haight-Ashbury dropout, who cares?

7

PLAYING SAFE

There is but one Game Rule that is inviolable: Goggles are a must.

If you do not wear goggles (or other suitable eye protection; more on that later), you will be eliminated from play. Furthermore, we know when you don't wear goggles. Each pair is equipped with a microtransmitter, which alerts our eye-guard computer when they are not worn. You can't spot it; it's molded in. When contacted, our computer calls your mother to tell her you are playing without adequate eye protection. Needless to say, Mom will be pissed.

That threat has a serious side. A marking pellet, smack in the eye, could blind. Be smart: Wear goggles at all times.

If you must remove your goggles during play, call out "Truce," place a white handkerchief on your head or around your arm, look around to make sure no one is drawing a bead on your brain, then remove your goggles and do whatever it is you have to do. Opposing players around you should honor your truce.

When you are done, replace your goggles, remove the handkerchief and vacate the premises.

The best type is industrial safety goggles with clear lenses and clear frames. We have experimented with different kinds and have found that those with ventilation ports, rather than ventilation holes in the frame, are least apt to fog. Treating the lenses with an antifogging compound is a good idea, and if you wear glasses, treat their lenses, too.

No matter how much antifog goop you put on, however, condensation will be a problem. You can control it somewhat by wearing a hat or headband to absorb sweat from your brow. And try not to overdress, to avoid working up a lather. No matter what you do, however, you probably will have to stop and wipe out your goggles from time to time.

The most successful alternative to goggles is a light-duty industrial shield—not a heavy welder's face guard, but a flip-down mask of Plexiglas most often worn as eye protection by people who operate grinders and metal-cutting machines.

Such a shield protects the entire face from a hit but has some drawbacks. Because it covers the mouth, it is apt to fog during fits of heavy breathing. Furthermore, it can be camouflaged only by covering

If you do not wear goggles, you will not play the Game.

it with tape, which cuts down on peripheral vision. Finally, such a shield makes you look like a third cousin of Darth Vader.

There is in the offering a Game helmet, a foam cap with ear protectors and a plastic face shield. It may prove to work well, but to my mind playing in such a rig is one step from showing up for a Game dressed like a hockey goalie. There has to be a little fear and pain (not in the eyes, of course), or play loses its zest.

For now, goggles work best. Wear them!

Other Parts May Enjoy It

What about protection for other parts, you ask (in a deep, husky voice). Most players do not bother with anything else. They wear baggy clothing, which takes most of the sting out of a hit, and go with the odds that they

A face shield is an alternative to goggles, but it must be taped to camouflage it.

won't take a splat to the crotch. But if you have an aversion to pain, mild as it may be, consider the following:

Groin: Baggy camo clothing over shorts or pants will absorb most of the hit, but if more protection is called for, wear a cup. It is that simple.

Bosom: A padded bra is the simple solution, or an unpadded bra wrapped with a bandeau made of handkerchiefs tied together. Several layers of shirts help. Potholders might work, too.

Neck: Tie a camo scarf or handkerchief around your neck. A headnet will help protect the neck, too. (A neck hit hurts about as much as anything.)

There is nothing else to worry about. I would rather be hit by a marking pellet at 10 yards than by a tennis ball on the fly. Or by a football on a cold day. Or even by a hard-thrown Frisbee. The most often used simile to describe a hit is that it feels like being popped by a towel in a locker room fight. That is inaccurate. I knew guys in high school who could take a piece of meat out of your leg with a well-rolled, slightly damp towel. A hit with a marking pellet—say, to the chest—feels like running into an overweight bumblebee while motorcycling at 58 miles per hour. That is, without the inevitable bee sting.

If you are worried about being hit, do this: Before you start to play, put your goggles on, hand your gun to a friend, and ask him to shoot you in the back at 10 yards. See, no big deal.

Wear eye protection, and you have nothing to fear.

But . . . heh, heh, heh . . . fear itself.

8

THE FIELD OF PLAY

No matter if you play on an official Survival Game field or in your back yard, the land—the game board, so to speak—influences the play of the game.

For example, in an Individual Game, 10 players sneaking around a 15-acre field may shoot each other up within minutes. Those same 10 players, however, on a 200-acre field may play out the Game without firing a shot. The size of the field profoundly affects the Game, and so do other aspects of the "playing board."

Size

Big fields emphasize woodsmanship, speed and stealth. Small fields emphasize tactics and, to a lesser degree, shooting ability. Now a big field can be 10 acres if only two people are playing, so the true indication of field size is player density: the number of players per acre.

As a rule of thumb, a Team Game with a player density of more than one player per two acres will be fast and furious. That means two teams of ten players each, playing on a 40-acre field, will shoot a lot (a total of 20 players on 40 acres equals a player density of one player for two acres. "He knows guns, he knows camouflage, he knows math!") Double the number of players and things get wild; double the acreage and fewer pellets will fly, yet the Game may be more challenging because strategy will assume more importance.

An Individual Game is a different creature. By its very nature an Individual Game has less shooting than a Team Game, although the shoot-outs can be more intense and more fun because encounters inevitably are one-on-one. The density rule of thumb for an Individual Game is about one player per five acres. Any Individual Game played on a field where the player density is greater than that (more than 10 players on a 50-acre parcel, for example) will have a good bit of shooting, but the more subtle elements of play will be lost.

Player density, naturally, is influenced by other factors, such as the type of terrain and the shape of the field. In open country the density should be decreased. In very thick country, say, in the middle of a jungle, player density might be increased with minimal effect on the Game.

Field Shape

Playing fields usually are delineated with surveyor's tape, that brightly colored plastic ribbon available at most hardware stores. There is no rule that says a playing field must be rectangular, round or any other shape. In fact, a poor playing area can be improved by laying out the boundaries in

Open woods are perfect for speedy players and for long-range shootouts.

an unusual pattern. For example, consider this rectangular field of 50 acres:

Fun, huh. Run from one end to the other. Straight-line stuff, not much challenge. But reconfigure the boundaries, and the Game changes. Consider the "U" shape:

This layout gives spectators a grand view of the action. It also necks down the field at the north end, ensuring some heavy shooting, and lengthens the playing area.

Now let's look at a really big field—150 acres:

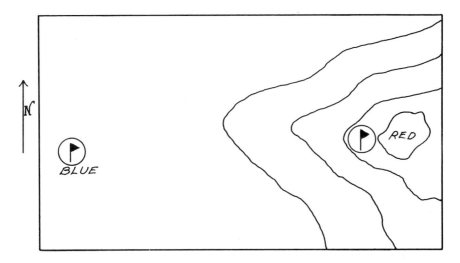

Set the "X" off center, and the red team's advantage of defending a flag on high ground is offset. Now the red team must converge as it approaches the blue team's flag:

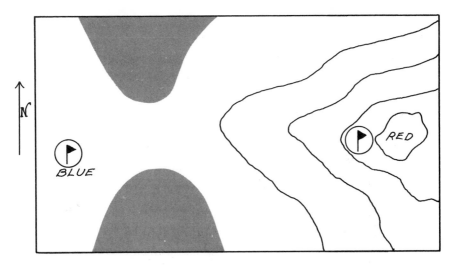

The field is open woods with high ground to the right. Neck down the field by laying the boundary in the shape of an "X," and the pitch of the game will increase:

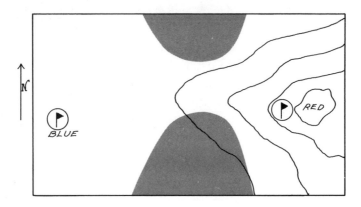

Options for field shapes are open. In designing a field, one must consider terrain, vegetation and the skill of players. It is much like laying out a golf course, except in the Game the field shape can be changed at any time, simply by reconfiguring the surveyor's tape. Plan the field first on paper, then string the tape. Stretching out a mile of surveyor's tape should take no more than an hour. Laying out a good playing field can be as challenging as playing the Game . . . almost.

Terrain

Terrain is a big factor. It determines a player's speed and course. No one in his right mind schleps through swamps. If a flag station is flanked by a swamp on its left, there is little point in defending it heavily on that side. (Naturally, there are exceptions. Some people will crawl through swamps.)

The principle elements of terrain are height and vegetation. Hills slow people down—or tire them out. On the way up or at the top of a hill, opponents are easier to shoot. Conversely, almost anyone can go down a hill at a good clip; and a person speeding along is a hard target to hit.

Vegetation has the same effects. Thick stuff slows people down. Thin cover is perfect for sprinting. But vegetation has another aspect: Vegetation can conceal, and that element of concealment can negate vegetation's influence on movement. For example, approaching a flag station slowly through thick cover may be preferable to approaching it quickly through open woods.

All this sounds elemental, but few Game players consider the influence of terrain on the play of the Game. And fewer people ponder how their opponents use terrain. Remember the example I used of a swamp on the left flank of a flag station? If my job is to defend that flag, I'm not going to

Terrain is a big factor. Few players would have the gumption to *shlep* through this wallow, wherein lives a rather large alligator.

pay much attention to that left flank. So a smart opponent like you might jump into that swamp and come up on my undefended side. Then *splat,* I'm done.

Here is another rule of thumb: Terrain has more overall effect on an Individual Game than it does on a Team Game. In a Team Game players must negotiate the terrain in both directions; that is, they must go from their flag station to their opponent's and then return to their station. So if they go uphill to get a flag, they must go downhill to bring it back. An Individual Game player, however, need not move in so structured a course. He might plan his route from flag to flag so that he would approach his last flag from high ground. Then, when he is tired and worn, he can call on gravity to zap him through the flag station on a dead-out run. Fast-moving player, difficult target.

Respecting the Residents

I know some Yankee game players who have practiced so much that I would bet on them against anyone, as long as they played up north. Put them in the South, however, and I might change my wager. The reason: There are what you call "residents" of fields in the South that can influence the way a person plays the Game. That is to say, one does not crawl about with gay abandon (as do my Yankee friends) when there are snakes around. Keep them in mind.

9

MODIFICATIONS AND TIPS

Rent a gun at a playing field or take one fresh from its box, slip into old jeans and a ragged shirt, don a pair of goggles and go on the field and win. The Game does not demand high technology. But there are a few extras that may be added to the kit, a few tuneups that can be performed on the gun that will increase the chance of winning, or at least increase the chance of not losing too soon.

The Gun

Game rules spell out permitted gun modifications (see Chapter 10). The National Survival Game, Inc. is not being pedantic in so doing, nor is it trying to stifle the inventive mind. Its concern is for player safety and equality.

Without strict rules, someone surely would add to the simple Nel-Spot a custom-machined 12-inch barrel extension, a $200 telescopic sight and a rifle stock. Then he would attach an oversized CO_2 cartridge charged 5,000 pounds to the square inch. The upshot would be a gun capable of repainting rainbows—the Game would go by the boards. Besides, someone might get hurt. So we have rules. They limit gun modifications so no one will be injured . . . or spend more than $2 tinkering with the gun.

Here, rule by rule, is what you can do to the Nel-Spot:

Tape the gun in any way you want, including use of camo tape, available at sporting goods stores or Survival Game dealers.

The camo tape is obvious: anyone who sees a Nel-Spot in the woods will figure that a player is attached to it. Camo tape will camouflage the gun. Tape also can secure the magazine cap to prevent it from falling out and spilling pellets over the woods.

Attach a rear magazine extender of not more than 10 inches beyond the rear end of the magazine.

A rear magazine extender is Game-ese for a cigar tube. At least that is what I have always seen sticking out from modified guns. The magazine extender serves two purposes. It enlarges the capacity of the magazine (or brings it back to standard capacity if a magazine plug is used) and it permits fast loading. Pellets carried in a cigar tube that press-fits to the magazine can be loaded simply by jamming the tube into the magazine and leaving it there.

Garcia y Vega tubes work well. Tubes from Cuban cigars are no more effective, but they show the player has good taste. Tubes from cheap cigars are reprehensible, particularly if the player actually smokes the cigars.

An alternative to a cigar tube is the plastic tube of the official Survival Game Pellet Pouch, on which more later.

The cigar tube extender and the Official Game pellet pouch.

Plug the magazine, but no modification is allowed that extends ahead or forward of the muzzle.

In loading the Nel-Spot, you may notice that as soon as a few pellets are fired and the magazine is no longer full, coaxing a fresh pellet to drop out of the magazine and through the loading port is difficult. Pellets roll around the tube like steel BBs in a pocket game. This problem occurs because the magazine extends ahead of the loading port. By blocking off the magazine in front of the loading port, one need only tip the gun forward. A new pellet will roll to the front of the magazine, hit the newly installed plug and tumble into the chamber. This simple modification drastically decreases loading and firing time. To make it, remove the plug from the front muzzle end of the magazine. Insert anything that is a tight fit and jam it down the magazine until it is flush with the front edge of the loading port. That's it. The National Survival Game sells (for a nominal fee) a special plug to save you the trouble of finding something else to fit down there.

Extend the bolt knob up to three inches.

Some people have difficulty cocking the gun. Lengthening the bolt handle by unscrewing and replacing the original with a three-inch hardened steel bolt makes cocking easier. There is a drawback, however: The extension catches on crud.

Modify the handgrips but do not enlarge them in any way.

You can carve your name in the grips or tape them up, just don't attach a rifle stock.

Modify CO_2 pressure screw as it extends from the butt.

Sometimes the ring on the end of the screw catches on a twig and backs off the screw. What follows is a rush of gas that sounds like this: *"Pssst!"* Then a rush of opposing players yelling this: "The fool's out of gas! Get him!" Then a rush of pellets that sounds like *splat*. You're out.

To prevent that, some players remove the ring. When they want to change CO_2, they stick a nail in the ring hole or just squeeze hard on the thing and twist. Roughing the protruding knob with a file makes it easier to grip.

Modify the first or front 1 inch of the inside of the muzzle, as long as that modification does not add to the pellet's velocity.

The thought behind this rule is that putting a slight spin on the pellet might stabilize its flight. To impart that spin, Bob Gurnsey, one of the Game's chiefs, conceived the idea of gluing a thin strip of light sandpaper on top of the inside of the muzzle. The sandpaper, Gurnsey reckoned, would impart backspin to the pellet, thereby lengthening its flight. Also, the sandpaper would scuff the pellet, so that it would rupture more easily on contact (this was conceived in the days before pellets were improved; it was not unusual then for a pellet to hit an opponent and bounce off).

Absolutely brilliant thinking, don't you agree? Well, the first time Gurnsey tested this logic, I happened to be standing next to him. He shot, and the pellet ruptured the minute it touched the sandpaper. We were facing into the wind, so all the paint came back on us in a fine mist.

Thereafter, this permitted modification has been known as the Gurnsey Goofball. No one can think of a sensible reason for modifying the first inch of the muzzle, but in honor of the short-lived Goofball, the rule still stands.

What else can one do to the gun? The question really should be, what else could one possibly want to do to the gun? If the sights are really off, a judicious nudge to the front blade with a small hammer might bring the sights back into line. If the pellets hit to the right, tap the front sight to the right. Hits to the left, tap to the left. The notch on the rear sight is very narrow for the width of the front blade, so judicious file work there to widen the notch might make the gun faster to aim. Any more tinkering with something that fires fat pellets filled with colorful guck falls under the heading of firearm fondling and should be discouraged.

Shooting the Gun

Several procedures will help you in play:

1. After shooting two tubes of pellets, change CO_2 as soon as possible. In the Game it is embarrassing to be low on gas. Better to have too much than too little.
2. For a long shot cock the gun twice. In other words, after chambering a pellet open the bolt, pull it back and push it forward again without permitting another pellet to enter the chamber. This double cocking puts an extra charge of gas into the gun, increasing range a bit.
3. Load two pellets into the chamber if you think you will be overrun by a scurvy hoard. Both pellets will fire. Sometimes however, one will rupture in the barrel. The double load is more of a psychological boost than anything else.

Gun Maintenance

Instructions for Repair, Replacement and Cleaning

A. Valve Assembly

1. Be sure to remove Enerjet No. 7-16.
2. Remove screw No. 7-27 and No. 7-13 to separate the Spacer-Frame Assembly (No. 7-17) from the rest of the gun.
3. With Small Allen wrench remove the 3 set screws (No. 7-15) to allow the Valve Body (No. 7-14) to be pulled out of the barrel (No. 7-2-3).
4. With Valve Body (No. 7-14) free from other mechanism insert a rod or thin screw driver through the (No. 7-13) screw hole at back end of the Valve Body to prevent it from turning while carefully unscrewing the Valve Seat (No. 7-8) from the opposite end.
5. Remove Valve Tube (No. 7-7) and Valve Spring (No. 7-11).
6. Unscrew Valve Cup-Seal (No. 7-10) from tube (No. 7-7)—examine for defect—clean or replace with new one.
7. Reassemble in reverse order. Be sure all parts are securely tightened and be careful not to damage or scar mating surfaces with the pliers or wrenches used. In replacing the Valve Seal (No. 7-8) be sure the "O" Ring No. 7-9 is in good condition and in proper position to make for an effective seal of the gas chamber.
8. In reinserting the Valve Body (No. 7-14) line up the protruding piercer with the Sear (No. 7-24) at the "Six O'Clock" position and insert and tighten the Set Screw (No. 7-5) at the "Six O'Clock" position first. Then insert and tighten the remaining set screws at the Ten and Two O'Clock positions.
9. Reattach Spacer-Frame Assembly (No. 7-17) by loosely inserting screws No. 7-27 and No. 7-13. Tighten the front screw No. 7-27 first.

B. Sear, Bolt Assembly, Hammer and Barrel

10. Proceed as above through step No. 6.
11. To remove Sear (No. 7-24), position it to expose tapered Sear Pin (No. 7-26) through holes on both sides of barrel. Insert proper size drive pin into hole of Hammer (No. 7-6) on right side (opposite Bolt Knob No. 7-28) and drive pin out, being careful not to lose Sear Spring (No. 7-25) located under rear end of Sear.
12. With pin and sear removed, Hammer (No. 7-6) will slide out of rear of barrel.
13. Remove Bolt Knob (No. 7-28) to allow Bolt Assembly (No. 7-4) and Main Spring (No. 7-5) to slide out. Special attention should be paid to condition of "O" Ring (No. 7-3). Any dried marking fluid should be removed with a strong solvent. If in good condition it may be reused, otherwise replace with a new one.

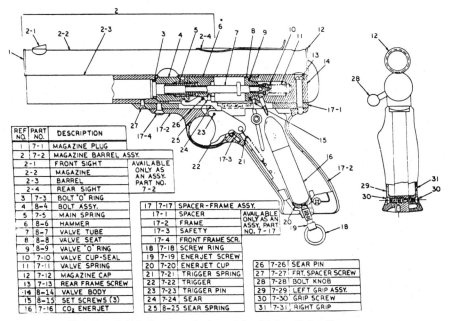

REF NO.	PART NO.	DESCRIPTION	
I	7-I	MAGAZINE PLUG	
2	7-2	MAGAZINE BARREL ASSY.	
2-I		FRONT SIGHT	AVAILABLE ONLY AS AN ASSY. PART NO. 7-2
2-2		MAGAZINE	
2-3		BARREL	
2-4		REAR SIGHT	
3	7-3	BOLT "O" RING	
4	8-4	BOLT ASSY.	
5	7-5	MAIN SPRING	
6	8-6	HAMMER	
7	8-7	VALVE TUBE	
8	8-8	VALVE SEAT	
9	8-9	VALVE "O" RING	
10	7-10	VALVE CUP-SEAL	
11	7-11	VALVE SPRING	
12	7-12	MAGAZINE CAP	
13	7-13	REAR FRAME SCREW	
14	8-14	VALVE BODY	
15	8-15	SET SCREWS (3)	
16	7-16	CO_2 ENERJET	

REF NO.	PART NO.	DESCRIPTION	
17	7-17	SPACER-FRAME ASSY.	
17-I		SPACER	AVAILABLE ONLY AS AN ASSY, PART NO. 7-17
17-2		FRAME	
17-3		SAFETY	
17-4		FRONT FRAME SCR.	
18	7-18	SCREW RING	
19	7-19	ENERJET SCREW	
20	7-20	ENERJET CUP	
21	7-21	TRIGGER SPRING	
22	7-22	TRIGGER	
23	7-23	TRIGGER PIN	
24	7-24	SEAR	
25	8-25	SEAR SPRING	

REF NO.	PART NO.	DESCRIPTION
26	7-26	SEAR PIN
27	7-27	FRT. SPACER SCREW
28	7-28	BOLT KNOB
29	7-29	LEFT GRIP ASSY.
30	7-30	GRIP SCREW
31	7-31	RIGHT GRIP

Reprinted with the permission of the Nelso Paint Company.

14. With all works removed, the Barrel can be cleaned of dried marking fluid by swabbing with a strong solvent or by stuffing barrel with solvent soaked rag; allow to stand for solvent reaction and then swab out loosened material.

15. To reassemble, proceed in reverse order. **Note:** When replacing Sear Pin (No. 7-26), drive it in from the left or bolt side. Care must be taken to insure proper positioning of Sear Spring (No. 7-25). When assembling Hammer (No. 7-6), the cavity (that accepts the Sear Spring) deep in the slot at bottom of Hammer must be toward rear of gun.

TROUBLE-SHOOTING GUIDE   NEL-SPOT "007" PISTOL

MALFUNCTION	PROBABLE CAUSE	CORRECTIVE ACTION
Gas leak from muzzle	Valve cup seal seating surface dirty, dented, or nicked.	Inspect seating surface with magnifying glass. Clean thoroughly if dirty, replace if damaged.
	Valve cup seal loose on valve tube.	Remove valve cup seal from valve tube, clean threads with wire brush, apply one drop Loctite Wick N' Lock to threads, reassemble valve cup seal to valve tube. NOTE: *Wipe excess sealant off seating surface of valve cup seal as soon as assembly is complete.*
	Valve O-ring swollen or bloated.	Remove and replace valve O-ring.
	Main spring too strong (overpowering valve spring when gun is uncocked)	Cut one loop from main spring, function check pistol. If problem persists remove ½ of next loop and function check again.

NOTE: *Whenever necessary to remove valve seat from valve body, clean inside valve body thoroughly.*

MALFUNCTION	PROBABLE CAUSE	CORRECTIVE ACTION
Gas leak in area around pin	Gas cartridge screwed in too far. (Past bevel on pin.)	Remove gas cartridge and replace with fresh one using care to not exceed ½ turn past the point when the pin pierces cap on cartridge.
	Burr on or near tip of pin.	Examine pin with magnifying glass; if burr is found, use india stone to restore pin to normal configuration.
	Pin loose or sealant broken on threads of pin.	Carefully unscrew pin, clean threads with wire brush. Use one drop Wick N' Lock on threads, and reassemble carefully, snug pin down firm. Note: *Wipe excess sealant off pin after assembly is complete.*

Problem	Cause	Corrective Action
Gun pops loudly when bolted back	Loose valve cup seal.	See corrective action for Valve cup seal loose on valve tube. Second corrective action.
Gun fires at the end of cocking cycle without trigger being pulled	Sear pin dragging on inside of barrel.	Tap sear pin into hammer far enough to eliminate possible drag.
	Sear hook deformed.	Remove and replace sear.
Gun difficult to bolt back when cocking	Sear pin dragging on inside of barrel. (Or lack of lubrication.)	Tap sear pin into hammer far enough to eliminate possible drag. Lubricate inside barrel.
Gun does not cock when cocking cycle is completed and gas pressure is adequate	Notch on bolt body has burr or is deformed or sear hook is deformed.	Examine bolt notch and sear hook for deformity. Use india stone to remove burr or small file to restore to normal configuration.
	Sear spring jammed or missing.	Examine sear spring and replace if needed.

NOTE: When removing parts from gun for replacement, *Do Not* discard old part. Old parts can be refurbished in most cases.

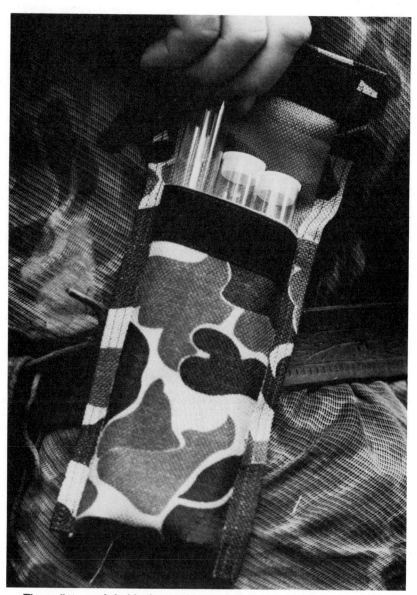

The pellet pouch holds three tubes of pellets. Tubes will press fit into the magazine of the gun to serve as a magazine extender.

At any Game, one will see a variety of headnets, face shields and costumes, but the use of such accessories is more a matter of personal style than anything else. Note the bolt extender on this gun.

Pellet Tips

Carrying pellets can be difficult. In the first Survival Game, most players stuck the cardboard tubes in which the pellets were packaged in their belts or pockets, and inevitably the tubes disappeared or pellets fell out. Things have come a long way since then.

The cigar tube was simply *de rigueur* until a few months ago. Hot players stuck their tube in the tops of their socks, then looped a rubber band around tube and leg. Some took things a step further and also taped a tube to the right side of their gun between the magazine and the muzzle. A taped tube and a leg tube identified the heavy shooters.

Recently, however, the Survival Game has come up with a pellet pouch, a nylon waist pack—in camo, naturally—that holds three plastic tubes. Each tube will carry 12 pellets and will press-fit into the magazine for quick loading. Now taping cigar tubes to one's leg is out of style.

What has not gone out of style since the first Game is the old pellet-taped-to-the-hand trick. By the rules of the Game, a player is out when he or she is marked. Don't say nothing 'bout havin' to be shot, now, do it. That means one can mark another player by swatting him with a pellet or by squeezing a pellet and squirting him with marking fluid. It works. Should one's gun malfunction, there is that pellet taped to the hand, ready for infighting. Just don't forget about it and slap a mosquito on your head.

What Else?

At any Game, there is a variety of headnets, face shields and costumes, but the use of such accessories is more a matter of personal style than of anything else. Excessive diddling takes something away from the Game. Inevitably technocrats will invent more goodies, but as far as I'm concerned, a pair of sneaks, goggles and a gun are all that are needed to have fun.

PLAYING
THE GAME

10

OFFICIAL RULES AND SUGGESTIONS FOR PLAYING

The Survival Game

The following suggestions and rules, for both the Individual and Team Survival Games, have been formulated to help standardize competition in those Games around the country. The rules given herein (along with any additions, deletions or changes National Survival Game, Inc. might decide to make) are the ones that will be in effect for all sanctioned competitions, including the national finals. Therefore, though you are of course free to play the Game any way you like, we urge you to play it according to the following rules and suggestions, so that you and your group or club can participate in sanctioned competitions. The rules and suggestions where safety is concerned *must* be followed, regardless of how you play the Game.

Suggestions for the Individual Game

1. Familiarize yourself with the pistol, the pellets and the goggles. Read carefully the information sheet on the pistol and pellets.

2. Get a group of more than six people together to play the game.

3. Get some people together to help with the Game, i.e. kids, spouses, wives, nonplaying friends. We recommend a total of seven helpers: four quadrant judges, an ultimate judge and two home-base keepers. What these people do is explained further on.

4. Choose a playing field. Though the game *can* be played almost anywhere, it is designed to be played on 20 or more acres of wooded land with varied terrain. As you increase or decrease the size of the playing field, the character of the Game changes, sometimes radically. (With 15 players on 20 acres, for instance, there will be a great many more shoot-outs than with six players on 100 acres.) Try to choose a field that is equally familiar or unfamiliar to all the players; ideally, for the first Game, it should be chosen, marked and mapped by the judges without the players entering it until the Game begins.

Be sure you have permission to use the land the field comprises.

5. Prepare the playing field. The playing field *must* be clearly delineated, either by natural boundaries (such as roads, streams, fields, trails, etc.), or by blazing trees with surveyor's tape. Wherever a natural boundary is used, it is up to the players to decide whether or not that boundary is to be included in the playing field—i.e. whether the trail, stream or whatever, *itself,* is in or out of bounds.

One or more of the judges, rather than players, should bound the field, and then divide it into four quadrants of roughly equal size. These four quadrants are called Red, Blue, Yellow and Green. On a tree central to each quadrant the judges should hang flags of a color matching that quadrant's name. These trees are known as flag stations. There should be as many flags at each station as there are players in the Game, and the flags should be hung from the tree so that they are *clearly* visible.

It is these four flag stations that should be manned by the four quadrant judges, one to a station, for the duration of the Game.

The judges should also locate two home-base stations. These stations can be at any two opposite sides of the field and should be located *outside* the nearest boundary by not more than 50 feet. During the Game, someone should remain at each home base to act as an official keeper and scorer.

Finally, the judges should locate and mark around the perimeter of the field evenly spaced entry locations, one for each player. These entry locations should be out of sight of each other and clearly marked by numbers pinned on trees (e.g. the numbers 1–12 for 12 players). Players should draw for their entry locations on the day before the Game.

After the field has been prepared as per the above instructions, the judges should make a rough map of the entire playing field (a topographical map overlaid with specific information is fine). The map should include major geographical features of the terrain and contour lines where possible, as well as the precise relative locations of (1) the four flag stations (2) the two home bases (3) the point in the field (it can be anywhere) to be occupied by the ultimate judge for the duration of the Game (4) the entry locations for players. The map should be Xeroxed and copies given out to the players not more than 24 hours before the Game begins.

6. The Game may be played more than once (in fact, many times) on the same field; but if it is, we recommend that you change the flag locations and the players' entry positions each time. We also suggest that at least one flag station be located in an open glade or field each time the Game is played.

7. Equip your judges. The judges should each have a whistle, if whistles are used (see below) and a good watch, and should wear a red or white shirt or jacket.

Your players should know how to work their pistols and how to read their maps and compasses, and they should be told what to do if they should happen to get lost. Your home base keepers should be thoroughly familiar with how to check a player for paint marks and with the scoring system, and they should have paper and pens for scoring and checking players out of the woods.

If some or all of your players are not very good with a compass, if you want a quick game, or if you are playing on a large piece of land, we suggest you supply your quadrant judges with whistles and have them blow prearranged signals every half-hour from the beginning of the Game till its end in order to help players locate the flag stations. If you want to be woodsy and pure about it, forget the whistles (they will not be used in the national finals); if you use them, assign each quadrant judge a different whistle signal (say, one long and three short blasts for Quadrant Blue) and identify these signals on each player's map.

On the day or night before the Game a meeting should be held for the players to review the rules and draw for their starting positions (it is a good idea to draw for the color dye each player gets, if different colored dyes are used).

8. Get everyone organized on the day of the Game. Get judges at their positions, home-base keepers at theirs, and players at their starting positions a few minutes before the Game's starting time. Starting can be done by the players themselves, having synchronized their watches and starting at an

agreed-upon time, or by starters, one per player, who start the players into the woods at the agreed time.

9. We suggest a three-hour time limit to the Game. If there is no outright winner in that time, first, second and third places should be awarded on the basis of points accumulated. The point system is explained in the Rules. Either your ultimate judge or your home-base keepers may be responsible for awarding points. We suggest you make it mandatory that home-base keepers check out *each* player at the Game's end, whether that player has a score or not, to insure not leaving anyone in the woods.

10. Final suggestions: Practice loading your pistols quickly as well as shooting them. Don't play your first Game on too large a piece of land. Never shoot at someone's face or head.

The Rules

1. Scoring. The point of the Survival Game is for a player to make his way into each quadrant, capture a flag from each of the four flag stations and escape from the field to one of the two home bases without being marked with dye by another player. The first player to do this within the Game's time limit is awarded 500 points and is the automatic winner of the Game.

In the event that within the Game's time limit no player wins outright as described above, the Game's winner, as well as second and third places, will be determined by the following point system. (If there *is* an outright winner, the point system still determines second and third places.)

Game Points

A. For each flag captured, a player is awarded 50 points.
B. For each "kill" (defined here as the elimination of another player by marking him with dye), a player is awarded 25 points.

Finishing Points

(These points are determined by the relative time of day at which a player with all four flags checks out of the Game with one of the two home-base keepers. For the awarding of these points it is important that a keeper write down the exact time at which each player with all four flags checks out of the Game).

A. The first player, unmarked with dye, to check out with all four flags is awarded a flat 500 points and is the automatic winner of the Game.
B. The second player, unmarked with dye, to check out with all four flags is awarded 100 points in addition to whatever Game Points he has accumulated. He may not, however, under any circumstances accumulate more than 450 aggregate Game and finishing points.
C. The third player, unmarked with dye, to check out with all four flags is awarded 50 points in addition to whatever Game points he has accumulated. He may not, however, under any circumstances, accumulate more than 450 aggregate Game and finishing points.

Tie scores for second and third places are possible and allowable.

2. A player who fairly marks with dye and thereby eliminates another player is free to take from the eliminated player his CO_2 capsules and/or dye pellets (these must be replaced after the Game). He may *not* take the eliminated Player's pistol or any flags that player might have captured.

3. In addition to Survival Game equipment, a player may take with him into the field *nothing other than* the following items: a knife; a length of cord or rope not to exceed 20 feet; camouflage hat, gloves, mask or netting; a pencil or pen and writing pad; a helmet or other head-protecting device; toilet paper; food and drink; insect repellent; tobacco; gum; personal medicines or drugs; matches and a pack.

4. If a player feels it necessary to carry with him anything not on this list, he must have the item or items approved by the ultimate judge at least 8 hours prior to the Game. If approval is granted the other players will be apprised and given the option to also carry the item or items.

5. *It is mandatory* that all players and judges wear the safety goggles provided by NSG, Inc. at all times during the Game. To ignore this rule could result in serious eye injury and possible loss of vision. It is also *strictly against* the rules of the Game to shoot anything from the pistols but the dye pellets provided; it is likewise against the rules to shoot those pellets frozen or in any condition other than that in which they are received. Failure to wear the goggles during the playing of the Game means instant disqualification.

6. A player may wear into the woods whatever he chooses, as long as his outerwear does not consist of more than a single layer of normal-weight clothing. If a player presents himself for scoring, he must do so dressed exactly as he was while in the woods, without having added or removed any clothing whatsoever.

7. A player may carry into the woods with him any number of dye pellets and/or CO_2 capsules, but no more than one pistol.

8. A player must retire from the Game immediately whenever that player is fairly marked, however slightly or indirectly, and at any place on the player's clothing or person, by dye belonging to another player. If a player should by accident mark himself with his own dye, that player is obliged to go immediately to the nearest quadrant judge for verification of the accidental self-mark. Any dye on the hands of a player (if it is the same color as the pellets issued that player or captured by him) will be assumed to belong to the player and does not require verification. If a player has not already captured a flag from the station to which he goes for verification of an accidental self-mark, he may not capture a flag from that station until after having captured one from at least one other station.

A player may mark, and thereby eliminate, another player either by shooting him, or by squirting or touching him with dye from a punctured capsule. Once a player has been fairly marked by shot, squirt or touch, that player is barred from marking the player who marked him. Should two players happen to mark each other simultaneously, either by shooting or by squirt or touching, both those players are eliminated. If a player is shot but not marked, by a pellet that fails to burst on contact, that player is still in the Game.

A player believing that he has marked and put out another player may call for a truce—by shouting the word "truce," and only that word—during which he may inspect the player suspected of being marked; if that player is marked he must leave the field; if not, the two (or more) players involved in the truce will walk out of sight of each other before resuming play.

If a player is marked by shot, squirt or touch and has no argument with his elimination, that player is obliged to leave the woods, report in to one of the two home bases, telling that judge the name of the player who marked him, and to remain out of the playing field for the duration of the Game.

If a player is marked by shot, squirt or touch and has legitimate argument with the method or fact of his elimination, he must immediately demand of the player who marked him an arbitration, and the player is obliged to grant it. In this event the two disputing players must walk as quickly and as silently as possible to the nearest quadrant judge for arbitration. If a quadrant judge's arbitration eliminates a player, that player must leave the woods immediately; if a Judge's decision returns a player to the Game, the judge will lead that player to a place in the woods which he deems appropriate and release the player there.

A quadrant judge may also opt to carry a dispute and its disputants to the ultimate judge for final arbitration.

9. Some symbol of neutrality (white handkerchief, vests or colored arm bands) should be shown by a player leaving the playing field, an accidentally self-marked Player, or two or more players in dispute.

10. A player is emphatically disallowed from shooting at any other player or players showing a neutrality symbol, or at any judge.

11. All judges should be identified as such by wearing red or white T-shirts or jackets.

12. A player may not leave the playing field at any time except to retire voluntarily and permanently from the Game, or in the case of his elimination.

13. In the event a player's pistol ceases to function or to function properly, that player is simply stuck with a nonfunctioning or dysfunctional pistol.

14. Any arbitration decision by a quadrant judge or the ultimate judge is inarguable and final.

15. No motor vehicle or bicycle may be used by a player at any time during the Game.

16. Only judges and players (and press members if they are wearing goggles) will be allowed within the perimeters of the playing field during the course of the Game.

17. No player may take with him into the playing field, or fashion while there, any object designed to function as a portable shield against being marked.

18. No mechanical or structural modification whatever of the dye pistols is allowed, with the following exceptions:

Allowed to tape the gun in any way you want including use of camo tape.

Allowed a rear magazine extender of not more than 10 inches beyond the rear end of the magazine.

Allowed to plug the magazine, but no modification is allowed that extends ahead or forward of the muzzle.

Allowed to extend the bolt knob up to three inches.

Allowed to modify the hand grips, but are not allowed to enlarge it in any way.

Allowed to modify CO_2 *pressure* screw as it extends from the butt.

Allowed to modify the first or front 1 inch of the inside of the muzzle, as long as that modification does not add to the gun's velocity.

No modification whatsoever which increases the velocity of the gun is allowed, including the use of any propellant more powerful than the standard 750 PSI CO_2 capsules presently used.

19. No player may shoot at another player who is outside the perimeters of the playing field.

20. During the course of the Game, quadrant judges, the ultimate judge and the home-base keepers are not allowed to give any information regarding the progress of the Game or the locations of flags to any player.

The penalty for breaking any of the above rules is instant disqualification from the Game in which the rule is broken and disallowance of any points accumulated in that Game.

Suggestions for the Team Survival Game

1. We suggest you limit the Team Game to two hours, and that the teams consist of more than six players each. If neither team has won a victory within the two-hour limit, the Game should be called a tie.

2. The Team Game can be played on any size or type of playing field, including fields devised in an urban environment, but, as with the Individual Game, it was *designed* to be played in the woods, on a field of between 20 and 100 acres.

3. You really only need two nonplaying helpers for the Team Game—a flag judge for each of the two flag stations.

4. We recommend that flag stations be located at opposite ends of the field and at least 100 feet inside the field from the closest boundary. Each team should be given maps prior to the Game indicating the locations of both team's flag stations.

5. The two team flags should be of different colors, and should be hung in fully exposed places, four to six feet above the ground.

6. The two flag judges should be equipped with Freon horns, or some other loud signaling device, for indicating when a Game has been won, and synchronized watches for noting the time at which a team claims victory.

The Team Game Rules

1. The point of the Team Game is for one team to capture the flag of the other team and bring it back to its own flag station. The first team to do this is the winner.

2. At the beginning of the Game each team must be assembled entirely at its flag station along with that flag station's judge. The team flag must be hung in plain view. No team member may leave his flag station until the agreed-upon time beginning the Game or until the sounding of the signal beginning the Game.

3. No team member may touch, alter the position of or mark with dye his team's flag as long as that flag remains at its station.

4. A flag may be recaptured from a capturing team (by eliminating the enemy player or players holding the flag); if such a recapture takes place, the flag must be immediately returned by its team to its exact original location at the team's flag station and the player carrying the flag must show a symbol of neutrality, granting him immunity from being shot or having the flag recaptured until it has been replaced in its original location, at which time the player returning it is back in the Game.

5. Any player carrying a flag, be it his own or the other team's, must wear the flag tied around his neck in plain sight.

6. Once any flag-carrying player is eliminated from the Game (marked with the other team's dye), he must immediately stop running or walking and *silently* give over the flag he is carrying to whomever on the opposite team demands it. Once a flag-carrying player is eliminated he may not in any way make it difficult for the opposing team to take his flag, and after the flag is given over he must leave the field immediately and silently.

7. Any member of a team may carry or capture the other team's flag, and that flag may be passed around among the members of the capturing team.

8. As for player elimination, all applicable sections of Rule #8 of the Individual Game apply here.

9. Rules 2–7 and 9–20 of the Individual Game also apply to the Team Game.

10. Either flag-station judge may be employed by either team at any time during the Game to settle legitimate disputes. A player or players approaching the other team's flag station for the purpose of settling a dispute with that flag-station judge may not fire their pistols or make an effort to capture the other team's flag until they have been taken at least 100 feet from the flag station by that judge and been released to continue play.

11

Basic Skills

Can't talk about the stuff any longer. Can't linger on the subtle psychological ramifications of the Game. Can't spend more time caressing the gun and taking deep breaths and stretching out tendons like a weekend marathoner. It is time to play, to get out there and grab a flag and pop someone, or get popped. So take to the woods, slink into the shadows. The ultimate challenge awaits, the challenge to *survive!* On the field of Survival Game play, roles will be written, men will become men and women women, the meek will inherit the earth, the good will dye young, and the first person shot will get to drink most of the beer. Profound, this Game. Now get the hell out there.

Getting Around

Lots of people who play the Game are whizzes on subways or at shopping-center sales but in the woods can't tell dogwood from dog breath. Furthermore, without street signs, they think they'll get lost. Not to worry. It is hard to get genuinely where-am-I lost on 100 acres (at most) circumscribed by gaudy surveyor's tape. So the first rule of getting around the woods is to forget about getting lost. Temporarily disoriented, maybe. But not lost.

The next thing to learn is how to read a map. Usually, players of Team or Individual Games are issued maps of the field. At best, maps are photostated from a topographical map, at worst they are copies of some third-grader's impressionistic scrawl of the woods. Maps at least should show the field's boundaries, the flag stations and the predominant terrain features: lakes, roads, streams, hills and the like.

All you have to do to read a map is: (1) figure out what is what, (2) figure out which way is up, (3) figure out where you are. From there on, life is easy.

Most markings are simple. Roads are lines, usually marked "Such-and-Such Road." Rivers are the same, marked "River," naturally. Swamps are marked with things that look like upside-down hairbrushes. In fact, on most Game maps, terrain features are quite obvious. Confusion may lurk only in the hair-thin lines that litter maps of hilly country, the contour lines.

Contour lines depict elevation. They are simple to read if you look at a map as a bird might view the country the map represents—from overhead looking straight down. Now realize that contour lines are imaginary lines on the ground connecting all the points of the same elevation. The difference between the elevation of each contour line is arbitrary and usually indicated on the map. For example, if the *contour interval* is ten feet, then the distance between two contour lines on the map represents an increase in elevation of ten feet. If you can't find that number, ask whoever is running the Game what the contour interval is. You may not know what you are saying, but you will impress the hell out of everyone else.

A few tips will help you make sense out of contour lines:

- The closer together the contour lines, the steeper the country.
- A closed contour line looking like a sick amoeba circumscribed by other contour lines represents the top of a hill.
- Contour lines stretching out in long fingers represent ridges.
- When contour lines cross streams, they form V's pointing upstream.

The accompanying illustration gives examples of these features. That is all you need to know about it.

Which way is up is easy. The top of the map is north, unless there is indication on the map to the contrary (such as a compass rose). If you have

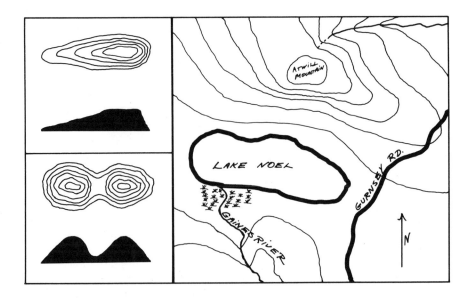

a compass, look at it. The needle or the "N" points north, too. So point the top of the map the same way the needle points. If you don't have a compass, remember this old woodsman's trick: The sun rises in the east and sets in the west. If it is morning, the sun is in the east. If the top of the map represents north, then the right side of the map represents east. Point the right side of the map toward the sun. If you can't see the sun or do not know what time it is, ask someone where north is. (That will impress the troops, too.) Then point the top of your map north.

Where you are is easiest yet. You probably are at the Game rallying area, which should be depicted on the map. Orient your map (top to the north, right side to the east, etc.). Look at the terrain features around you and the features depicted on the map. The same, right.

You're a woodsman.

Now that you know how to read a map, using a compass will be a snap. The compass most often used in Game play and sold by the National Survival Game, Inc. is of the pin-on variety. It is a small plastic sphere encapsulating some mysterious liquid wherein floats a magnetically charged ball. On the ball are printed the cardinal points of the compass. Attached to the back of the plastic sphere is a safety pin.

To use this compass or any other, look down at the floating ball. Note there is an arrow (or "N" for north) on the ball. That arrow points north all the time. It is never wrong, unless you should stand within the magnetic field underneath high-tension power lines, on top of a large iron deposit or with a hunk of metal (your pistol, for example) near the compass. So keep your pistol and all metal away from your compass.

To travel north, turn your body until you face in the direction the arrow points. That applies even if you are not using a pin-on compass. The key, remember, is to turn yourself. Don't just spin the compass around in your hand, as many people are apt to do.

Now try another direction, say southeast. That is halfway between south and east, so turn your body until you are on line with the point halfway between south and east. You now are heading southeast. As you move, keep your body aligned with the southeast mark on the compass. If things go askew, don't try to compensate by cocking your head to look at the compass from another angle or by twisting the compass off your shirt. Change your direction of travel. That is all you need to know.

If you have heard about the other mysteries of compasses—declination angles, back azimuths and the like—forget them. You are not navigating across the Sahara; you're trying to find a flag on 100 acres of ground.

With that sound advice stored away, you are ready to use your compass and map together. Say you are playing an Individual Game. Your starting position is marked on the map at Point A.

You intend to capture the blue flag first. To determine your direction of travel, approximate the compass direction from your position to the flag.

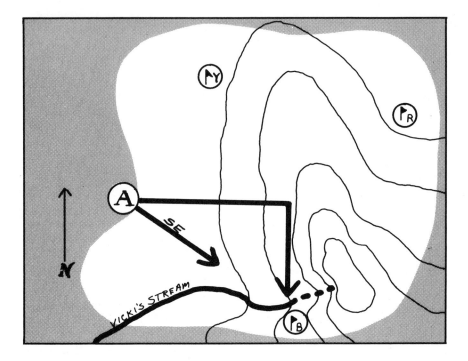

Remember that the north–south line is parallel to the side of the map, north at the top and south at the bottom. That puts east on the right, west on the left, and all points in between. A straight line from your starting position to the blue flag runs toward the right-hand side of the map, toward the east. But that line is not parallel to the top of the map. It slants down somewhat, toward the south. Therefore, your direction of travel is southeast..

You don't have to be more accurate than that in the Survival Game. In fact, you will find that once you have spent some time in the woods, you will forget your compass and just watch terrain features to find out where you are. Look at our example again. Note that the blue flag station is against the side of a ridge and next to a small stream. If you set out from your starting position and head roughly east, you will hit the ridge. Then, if you turn right and follow the ridge until you hit a stream, you will find the flag station.

There is a great deal more to be learned about navigating, but the Game is not the place to acquire such skills. Reason: If you are paying too much attention to your map and compass, you may well forget to be on the lookout for the bad guys in the woods. Then *splat*.

Moving

Once you know where you are going in an Individual or a Team Game, you must decide how to get there. Walk? Run? Slink? The speed at which you move depends on your strategy, but the way in which you move is a function of how badly you want to be shot.

Fast or slow, you should keep two things in mind: cover and concealment. Concealment to hide you from the bad guys, cover to protect you from their pellets if the concealment doesn't work.

If you decide to move slowly, put more emphasis on concealment. Plan every step of your movement. If you are behind a tree, find another tree a few yards away to which you can move. Go from tree to bush to shadow to ferns to high grass in deliberate steps. Don't get caught in the open. If you choose to move slowly, move slowly. Very slowly. Slower than that.

If you choose to move slowly, move very slowly—a few steps at a time.
If you spot a bad guy, freeze.

Slowly, a few steps at a time. And if you spot a bad guy creeping through the woods and cannot find a handy shadow or clump of crud to hide in, then freeze. Don't move anything. Chances are good that you will not be spotted.

If your strategy is to move fast, look more for cover—hard things that will stop pellets: rocks, trees, logs and the like. If you come to an open area, cross it quickly after watching for a while to see if there is someone lurking nearby. And if you cannot clear the area in one bound, remember that cover and concealment lie at your feet. *Hit the dirt and flatten out.* If you are well camouflaged, you will be hard to spot. If you scrunch down enough, you will be harder to hit.

Cover and concealment are the keys to getting around.

When Push Comes to Splat

But say you screw up anyway. You are spotted. *Splat,* a pellet hits to your left. You dive behind a log. *Splat,* another shot. Oh, God, I didn't know it would be like this, you think. What to do?

You have two choices: attack or retreat. Most new Game players default on both and lie there, praying for divine intervention or Mom's soothing call: "Come in the house now, Johnny, it's time for lunch." But neither comes.

Cover and concealment lie at your feet. If you are spotted in the open, hit the dirt and flatten out.

Whether you attack or retreat is a function of your personality and the circumstances. Aggressive people play aggressively; rarely do they pass up a chance to shoot it out. But that does not mean attacking is always the proper thing to do. Naturally, if the person shooting at you is one of seven opposing players facing you, discretion is the better part of valor—which means haul ass.

Retreating is a minor art. One should not retreat pell-mell; rather, the retreat should be planned much like forward movement, although the time available to contemplate each move is diminished. Retreat in bounds from cover to cover. Make the bounds very fast. Very fast. Do not retreat along a predictable route, but zigzag off to safety. If you are engaged by one opponent, shoot at him before moving, even if you cannot fire a good shot. The *splat* will keep his head down for a second, and in that time you should be halfway to your next cover. If an entire gang has you pinned, best to save your shot for when you get to your next cover, for inevitably when you move, someone will come after you. If you are prepared to shoot as soon as you reach cover, you may catch him in the open. Then the odds are reduced.

The minute you have maneuvered out of effective range, 30 to 40 yards, run like hell. And hide, which means finding concealment, trusting your camouflage and not moving an inch.

But what if the *splat* comes from one player—your boss, perhaps—and you cannot resist an attack? You have several options.

New players tend to hold their position and shoot and shoot and shoot until someone retreats, quits, runs out of pellets or is hit.

Experienced players opt to maneuver on an opponent. An experienced player will work from cover to cover, closing the distance. He may intentionally draw fire; then, in those seconds when his opponent is cocking his gun, he charges and shoots. *Splat.*

The key is timing. An average player can reload in about three seconds. An average player can get up and run maybe 10 yards in three seconds. An average player can hit another player 90 percent of the time at 10 yards. Those are the average factors. Apply them to a shoot-out and the scenario would look like this:

Player A and Player B are 40 yards apart when A shoots at B, who hits the ground. A (for aggressive), runs forward five yards as B squirms for cover. B shoots at A. A immediately shoots back and runs forward another five yards. They are now 30 yards apart.

Player A has little cover, so when B shoots at him, he sprints laterally to the safety of a big rock. B still has not moved. A draws fire, returns fire and dives forward to the safety of a log. The players are now 25 yards apart.

Player A now is in good position to charge. He waits for B to shoot, then moves in. Within three strides he is 12 yards from B with a clear shot. He draws a bead and fires.

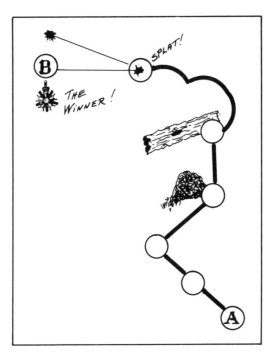

Unfortunately, A is a terrible shot. He misses and B wastes him with a drilling to the belly. So it goes. Nevertheless, A had a lot of fun and should have been the victor in the battle had he been able to hit anything.

There is one other offensive move that all Game players come to learn—and love. It is called the *Pssst* Charge, so named from the sound of CO_2 gas escaping from a cylinder.

From time to time in almost any Game, someone either will accidentally release the gas in their gun—hence a loud *Pssst*—or run out of gas and be forced to change cylinders. When a used cylinder is removed, the small amount of gas remaining in it escapes, again producing a *Pssst*.

Hearing that sound, an experienced player knows that his opponent ain't got nothin in his gun. Nice guys then rush and shoot their victim. Really evil, slimy players just walk in slowly, jam their gun in their opponent's ribs (or neck, or . . .) and demand surrender.

There is one thing to be aware of, however. A few old pros can do a fine imitation of a *Pssst*.

The Ambush

The final offensive element of Team or Individual play is the ambush, a situation in which one player in hiding has the opportunity to splatter another player, unaware of his opponent's presence. Sounds easy, but things often go wrong.

The ambusher must remain still and undetected until the ambushee is well within range.

The ambusher must remain still and undetected until the ambushee is within painting range. That means about 10 to 15 yards. Any closer and a miss or a malfunction spells instant splattering for the ambusher; his intended victim has him cold before he can reload. An earlier shot risks a miss, and the advantage of the ambush is lost.

The ambushee, when ambushed, has but one course of action, assuming he is not out of the game: Attack. If missed, the ambushee has the upper hand, for the ill-intentioned sleaze who hoped to splatter him unaware now must reload. And remember that reloading takes several seconds, enough time for ambushee to charge and dispatch.

Basic Game skills are common sense. If you cannot remember what to do, keep a cool head. The kicker, of course, is that keeping a cool head when someone is lobbing paint at you and yelling threats about redecorating your face is often hard to do.

So if all else fails, remember this: You can always throw up your hands and shout, "I quit!" Surrender is not a dirty word in the Game. Should someone chastise you for bailing out, look him or her squarely in the eyes and call him or her an anal retentive, neo-Nazi deviate.

That will shut almost anyone up.

12

THE INDIVIDUAL GAME

The Survival Game was conceived as an Individual Game. The Team version followed. Although the majority of Survival Game players consider the Team Game more fun, the Individual Game is more challenging. There are as many variables in an Individual Game as there are players—factored by the intricacies of each player's mind, time, terrain, weather and the amount of beer available for consumption following play.

Because of the complexity of an Individual Game, set tactics have less effect than in a Team Game, where players, although individuals, function predictably as a group. A Team Game is checkers, an Individual Game is chess. Team players must proceed from their flag to their opponents' flag and back to their flag. An individual player may dash for one flag then lurk for an hour, may move in a straight line or a corkscrewed path, may go after the four flags in any order or may decide not to win—in the conventional sense of amassing points—and concentrate on shooting other players.

Patterns of Play

Patterns of play emerge, however. Examining them can give a new player suggestions for his actions and a glimmering of insight into the tactics of others.

A Sneaker won the first Survival Game. A Sneaker is a player who assiduously avoids contact with other players. A Sneaker proceeds slowly and methodically from one flag to another, always counting on spotting an opposing player before that player spots him. In turn, a Sneaker will hide until his opponent passes by.

A Sneaker will take several hours to collect his flags. He compensates for his slow movement by not shooting at anyone, even if he has a chance to splatter another player clean as can be, because he recognizes that a shoot-out is the most time-consuming aspect of a Game.

A Sneaker must be a woodsman. He must know how to read a map and compass, move slowly and hide. Libras make bad sneakers.

A Team Game is checkers; an Individual Game is chess. The ability to stop and weigh options is all-important.

The Nike Ninja counts on speed. Often his previous exposure to the woods was a mugging in Central Park. His tactic is to run like a somabitch, snagging flags along the way. Because he finished ahead of three guys in wheelchairs, a 12-year-old girl and a dog of mixed breed in a mini-marathon, he is confident his speed and endurance will see him through. People may shoot at him, but lucky will be the player who gets him.

The Nike Ninja's tactic is not bad. A fast-moving target, you will remember, is hard to hit. Unless he is well ambushed, the Ninja may succeed. The two stumbling blocks he faces are underestimating the difficulty of running through the woods full tilt and succumbing to the lure of stopping for a shoot-out. In shoot-outs, Nike Ninjas rarely win.

The Nike Ninja counts on speed. A fast-moving target is hard to hit, and unless he is well ambushed, the Nike may succeed.

Play-It-By-Ear is the average Individual Game player. The Ear will attempt to stick it in the ear of any opposing player he encounters, but he will not lose sight of the objectives—the flags. He is an opportunist. When he comes to open woods and has enough wind to see him through, he may sprint for 100 yards. In dense growth he may sneak and crawl. At the bottom of a draw that might funnel players coming off a hill, he may hide and wait for prey.

The Ear is most flexible, yet his flexibility can get him in trouble. Because he will stop and shoot, because he will sneak from one flag to the next, then run in a spectacular spurt and inevitably push himself to the brink of a heart attack (necessitating a 20-minute break with a couple of cigarettes and an illicit beer), the Ear wastes time. Ears have fun, but rarely win. Fortunately, they don't care.

Death Doctors, named in honor of Bob Carlson, the physician who played in the first Survival Game, do not care about flags. Nor do Death Doctors care that they do not care about flags or that other people may think they nurture latent homicidal tendencies and fascist leanings. Death Doctors are supremely confident in their motivation. Death Doctors play for fun.

Death Doctors just love to shoot people. They do so by lying in ambush and by actively looking for other players. Often they will hide near a flag station and paint players as they come in, or they will prowl the playing

The Ear is an opportunist. He may hide and ambush other players for a while, then spring for 100 yards to the next flag.

Death Doctors love to shoot people. They never win an Individual
Game, but they have so much fun, they never lose, either.

field looking for predictable lanes of travel through which a victim may pass.

Needless to say, Death Doctors never win either. But for all the fun they have, they never lose.

Individuals at Play

Those four patterns play out against a backdrop of many variables: the starting positions of other players and their possible routes and patterns of play, terrain, layout of the field, flag locations, time, the physical and mental condition of the player, and other things I haven't even thought of.

To see how factors interrelate, let's look at the playing field of a classic Individual Game, one that shall be remembered in Survival Game history with the awe and reverence historians hold for such key military battles as Midway, the Bulge, and Bull Run. The First (please, bow your head) Survival Game.

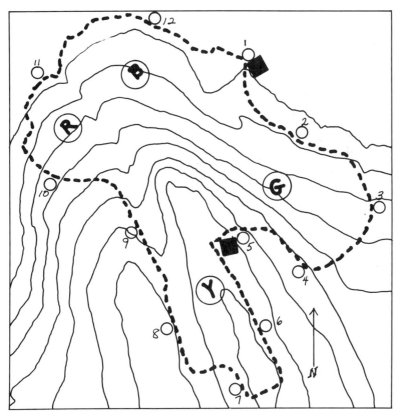

Individuals at Play

Here is the field. It encompasses 125 acres of New Hampshire woods. The boundary is irregular and delineated by a trail. A large ridge running approximately north–south dominates the terrain. The flag stations, marked R, B, G and Y for red, blue, green and (you guessed it) yellow, lie in four quadrants. The closest flags, blue and red, are 600 feet apart; blue and yellow are furthest apart, about 2100 feet. The contour interval, the elevation gain or drop between contour lines, is 40 feet. The starting positions of the 12 players are marked by small circles around the periphery of the field. The base stations are indicated by black boxes.

Players used every pattern in that first Game (although we did not know it then). To avoid embarrassing anyone, I have exercised some artistic license by fictionalizing strategies—and the outcome, specifically the part where I win.

The Sneaker at Play

The Sneaker starts on the western side of the field at Position 10. Because sneaking is his nature, he probably would sneak no matter where he starts, but sneaking lends itself to this position. The player to his north at Position 11 probably will rush the red flag. Although that player must go uphill and the Sneaker can go downhill, the Sneaker guesses there is a good chance both would arrive at the flag about the same time. So that rules out an initial rush for the Sneak. He starts off slowly, allowing the player to his north plenty of time to get through the red flag station and be on his way.

With the red flag in hand, the Sneaker plans to approach the blue flag from the north. Only one other player, Number 12, probably would come from that direction, and by the time the Sneaker reaches that flag, Number 12 should have passed through.

The same thinking holds for the green flag. Most of the players will approach the flag from the west side, so the Sneak will hug the boundary and take it from the east.

The final flag is the most difficult. The Sneaker reasons he should move up the middle of the playing field so that he will have room on either flank to maneuver. When he gets the yellow flag, he will slink to the nearby base station. The Sneaker allots two hours to collect all four flags.

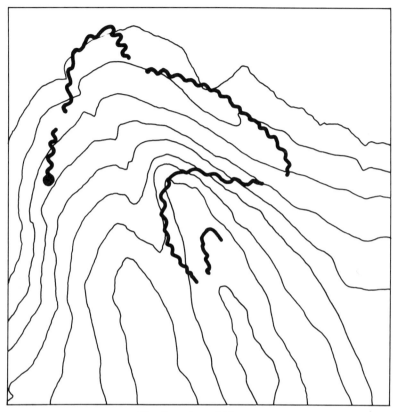

The Sneaker at Play

The Nike Ninja at Play

Nike starts as close to the yellow flag as anyone. Furthermore, that station is downhill from his position, so by sprinting he should be through and on his way to the next flag before anyone else approaches. He plans to swing wide around Position 5, then head downhill to the east toward the green flag. From there he will cut cross-country to the red flag. Note that on all legs the Nike will be running downhill or on the level. From the red flag, he will sprint to the blue, then to the nearest base station.

His fleet-footed tactic works particularly well from his starting position. He is on high ground. He is close to his first flag. Except for the sweep he must make around Position 5, where he comes close to the boundary line and risks being trapped between it and another player, he sticks to the middle of the playing field so he has plenty of running room.

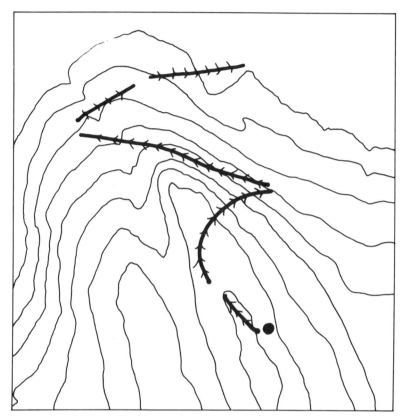

The Nike Ninja at Play

Play-It-by-Ear at Play

The Ear is *soooo* crafty. He has everybody figured out. He will spring to the green flag, take it and drift to the south side of that station and ambush player 4. Then the Ear will sneak uphill to the top of the ridge and set up another ambush. He hopes to take out a couple of players moving toward the yellow flag. If he succeeds, the narrow part of the field around the yellow flag will be less congested.

Next, the Ear will switch into his Nike guise and run like hell out of that neck to the red flag. From there he will sneak to the blue flag. Stealth, he reasons, is necessary now because the red and the blue flags are close together, and many players will be around that part of the field. From the blue flag, the Ear will shag off the field to the base station near Position 1.

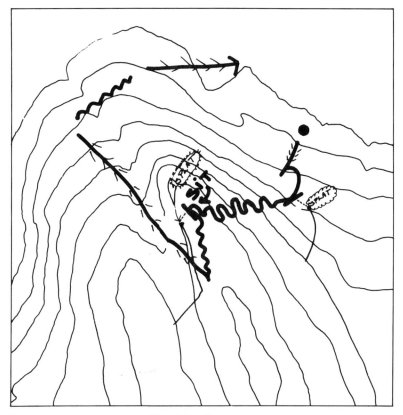

Play-It-by-Ear at Play

Death Doctor at Play

The Death Doctor's plan is to head immediately for the neck of the field. There he should find the meat he craves. He will set up an ambush in the hope of splattering all the players from the most southern starting positions and any others heading south to the yellow flag.

After 30 minutes or so, he plans to go north to the blue station and ambush that flag. Then he will meander around the middle of the field in search of trouble. Finally, he will head south and ambush the yellow flag station. His theory is that since the yellow flag is the most difficult (the station is uphill and the field around it is constricted) the smart players will leave it for last. And that is when the Death Doctor will get them.

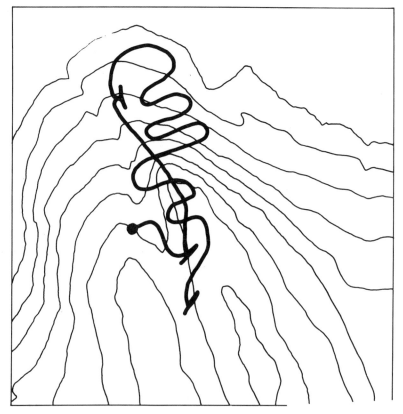

Death Doctor at Play

Those are the plans of four players. All are sound. However, there are eight other players on the field, and each of them also has a plan, variations and combinations of the four basic styles of play. Diagram them all, and the outcome looks like this:

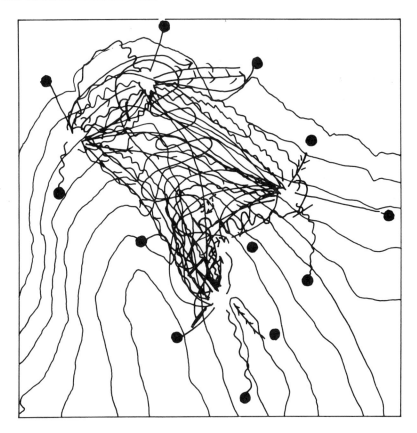

Now that explains things, doesn't it?

Ah, but it does. It demonstrates that the greatest variable in any Individual Game—the one variable that cannot be factored prior to play— is the actions of other players. Unlike Pac-Man, the opposition is not programmed. One can count on meeting another player sometime in a Game, and one can plan a generalized tactic: The Sneaker and the Nike will avoid conflict by hiding or running. The Ear may run, hide or fight. The Death Doctor will stand his ground. But one cannot predict when an encounter will take place or what the other player will do.

That means flexibility within any pattern of play is most important, flexibility to change routes or even one's favorite pattern. If an hour into a

Game a confirmed Sneaker sees that he is spending all his time hiding because the player density is high and the woods are crawling with Death Doctors, he may be forced to abandon his preferred pattern and haul ass like a Nike.

That is the appeal of an Individual Game. Few of us have the chance in everyday life to experience immediately the consequences of our actions. The Game provides that chance. Decision follows decision: Run, turn north, shoot it out, go for a flag, hide, give up. In an Individual Survival Game, whatever decision we make, the consequences are here, now: a flag, a win, a *splat* in the back.

Besides that, the Game's a hell of a kick.

Individual Game Player's Checklist: Factors to Consider

Before Play

Opponents' Positions: How close is nearest player? Are other players close to your first flag? Is a known bloodthirsty fascist with a yearning for your head anywhere around?

Opponents' Possible Routes: Will the the terrain or the shape of the field channel other players across your route? Will other players be heading toward you because you are near a flag? Do you know the preferred pattern of play of adjacent players?

Terrain: Uphill or downhill to first flag? Other flags? Will vegetation (open woods, dense woods, swamps, etc.) have an effect on speed and visibility? Is vegetation suitable for hiding?

Flag Locations: What is the distance between flags on your proposed route? Which flag is most difficult (because of terrain or field boundaries)? Best, perhaps, to save that flag for last when player density will be reduced? Will any flag be hard to find?

Field Layout: Is one part of field more dangerous than the rest (does field neck down, squeezing players together)? Is last flag station on proposed route near a base station?

Weather: Raining—will footing be bad, visibility poor? Sunny— should you consider approaching flags with sun to your back so players to your front cannot spot you as easily as you can spot them?

During Play

Players Remaining: Can you estimate players left (starting number minus those you have shot minus those others may have shot)? Have you eliminated any players with known skills or patterns?

Time Remaining: Look at watch.

Flags Remaining: Count number of flags in hand. Subtract from total number of flags.

Condition: Yours—are you out of breath, suffering from tightness in the chest? Are your limbs cold, your eyes immobile and your breath nonexistent—might you be dead? CO_2 and pellets remaining? Gun functioning properly?

What are you waiting for? Go.

13

THE TEAM GAME

The Team Game is what people talk about, and the Team Game is what people want to play. The Team Game lacks some of the intensity and complexity of the Individual Game, but those shortcomings are compensated for by the camaraderie that infuses a Team Game, by the heightened pace of play and by all the shooting that inevitably goes on.

Now I'll admit it, the Team Game is a little like war. Just a little, mind you, because the analogy is fragile. It exists only when one element of war is considered, and considered out of context.

That element is the planning of strategies and tactics, the analytical thought necessary to take objectives. Viewed abstractly, such detailed planning can be challenging, even fun—much like a Team Game.

Planning for war, real war, is not abstract, however, and most planners on every level, from PFCs to generals, carry out their jobs burdened by the knowledge that their actions will lead to suffering and death. Therefore few, if any, find fun in what they do. I deliver that sobering sermon so that you will not think I consider the Survival Game to be a pantomime of war when I say, *Look to the Army if you want to win a Team Game.*

The Army, you see, has refined tactics to a science. It has reduced the planning necessary to capture a hill—or a flag—to beautifully tabulated paragraphs, subparagraphs and sub-subparagraphs. The Army may move on its stomach, but before it moves it inevitably makes lists of where it is going and how many bellies will be along.

The Army's outline of how to take a hill (or anything else worth taking) is called a Five Paragraph Field Order. In a Team Game, two of those paragraphs are extraneous, since the *mission* in a Team Game is always the same—to capture the other guys' flag—and the *administration* and *logistics* of a Team Game amount to seeing that everyone has pellets and knows where the beer is stashed at the end of the Game. By the same token, many subparagraphs do not apply to Team Game play; as yet no one has seen a need or figured out how to call in artillery or naval guns.

So the working field order of a Team Game is reduced to this:

1. Situation
    a. Enemy
    b. Terrain
    c. Location
    d. Friendly
2. Execution
    a. Concept
    b. Missions of Elements, Teams and Individuals
    c. Coordinating Instruction
        1. Departure Time
        2. Formation and Order of Movement
        3. Routes and Alternate Routes
        4. Rallying Points
        5. Action on Contact
        6. Action at Danger Areas
        7. Action at the Flag
3. Command and Signal

Simple, huh?

Don't panic. None of it is necessary, really. A team can say, "Let's get 'em," and everybody roars off for the opponents' flag with nary a thought to strategy. No one can say they will have less fun, but there is a good chance that if they are playing an organized team, they will lose. So the effort of planning strategy in a Team Game is important, if you want to win. (Which brings up an interesting point. There is an adage that goes, "If winning isn't important, why keep score?" Great adage, that. Funny thing, though, I have never attended a Survival Game where anyone keeps score for more than 30 seconds.)

Let's look now at each element of that plan. In so doing you will discover much about Team play and the variables involved.

Situation

Know your *enemy* is the first rule. If the other guys like to sprint for flags, take that information into account when planning your strategy. If they like to ambush, consider that. Look at the playing field from their perspective. Do they face a hill at the start of the Game? If they do, they may decide not to attack your flag aggressively.

Analyze the *terrain* of the playing field. Does it neck down at one point? Is the vegetation particularly thick? Are there open areas that will be dangerous to cross?

Proper planning of strategy is the key to winning a Team Game.

Consider the *location* of your opponents' flag. Can it be approached from several directions, or is it backed up against a boundary or natural obstacle? Is it on the top of a hill? How would it best be defended?

Finally, look at your team, the *friendlies*. Bunch of hard-assed, fit, ex-commandos? Or a quintet of quiche eaters? Who is playing, what kind of shape they are in and the makeup of their personalities must be analyzed before you come up with a scheme.

Execution

Here, friend, is where you have to do some thinking. There is no right answer. The best guidance I can give is this: keep it simple. If you plan some compound flea flicker of a play, with maneuvering elements approaching the flag from several directions and defenders staggered all over the field in a complex variation of the Miami Dolphins' old 5–4 defense, you are going to get wiped. Complex plans fall apart seconds after the whistle blows.

It you can't sum up the *concept* of your plan in a sentence, then you will be in trouble. It should sound something like this: "We're gonna defend until we blast half their guys, then we sprint to the flag." Or . . .

"We're gonna run like hell down the side of the field, take their defenders by surprise, then shag back here." Or . . .

"We're gonna send one group to ambush that field, and the other group will slowly work up the edge toward their flag. Six men back to defend the flag." Or the most famous concept of all . . .

"High-diddle-diddle, straight up the middle."

Believe me, there are just so many ways to get a flag at one end of a field and bring it back to the other end of the field. You court disaster if your plan sounds like the following.

"Element A will depart 13 seconds after Element B, circle around the far side of that open area to make the other team think that we are going to ambush them from their left flank. Meanwhile Element X will run downfield 200 yards, then hold as a reserve for Element T, which must set up a diversionary defensive position 27 yards past the primary defense, Element M, providing that Element A does not encounter resistance of more than 27 percent of the opponent's projected advance element reacting to the ambush of Element B set up on a tangent to the line of advance of the scout patrol, which will be going out before Element B but after Element A. . . ."

Keep it simple: Defenders to protect your flag, attackers to get their flag, maybe an ambush to tip the odds, possibly scouts to see what the other guys have waiting. How you weigh those four elements can alter the concept of your game. For example, you may decide to put everyone on defense for an hour in the hope of wiping out the other team. But sometime you will have to get the other flag, and that brings us back to an attacking group, even though there may be no more opposing players to attack. Simple, simple, simple.

Simple, because great Games, like great battles, are not won on complex concepts but on efficient *execution*: How well elements, teams and individuals work together.

Elements are the groups on a Team that must carry out certain tasks. The primary elements are *defenders, attackers, ambushers* and sometimes *scouts*.

Defenders, naturally, are charged with defending the flag. In almost any Team Game, at least two players are designated as defenders. Between them they may decide that one player should cover the flag and hold his fire, so as not to give away his position, until an opponent actually rushes the flag. The other defender may position himself along the opponents' likely avenue of approach and start shooting the other guys as soon as they come within range. For example:

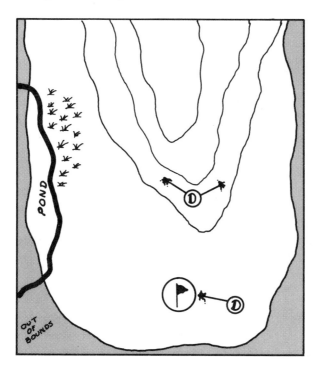

If more defenders are assigned, their execution may be more complex. For example, two defenders may cover the flag, two may take up forward

positions to fire on the bad guys when they can and two others may go
forward 100 yards or so with the plan of shooting at the opposing team
when they come into range, then dropping back to a second defensive
position:

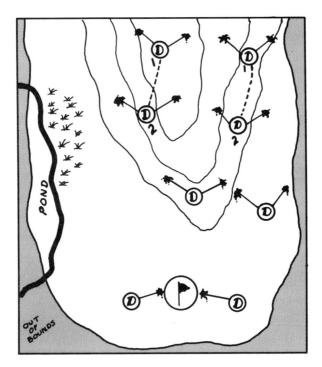

What defenders do and how many do it are determined by the number of
players on the team, the terrain, the concept of the plan and the anticipated
strategy of the opposition. Sometimes all those factors are thrown out the
window when everyone on the team is over 35, and no one has the strength
or ambition to shag down the field and attack. In such a case, everyone
plays defense.

If defenders make one error, it usually is this: They shoot too soon and
give away their positions. A defender should not fire unless he is certain
that he will take out an opponent. Then he has two options. If he is well
concealed and protected, he may hold his ground. Otherwise, he should
consider falling back to another, preselected position, from which he can
take out another player. Thus,

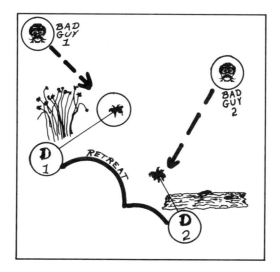

Finally, defenders must consider what they will do if and when the opposing team gets their flag. They may choose to leave the field and get a beer, or they may opt to pursue the opponents, flank them and set up an ambush, pass them and go for their flag, or scream in unison for their attackers to be on the lookout for the other guy running down the field.

Attackers are the glamour boys. Attackers go for the flag, but attackers also get blasted, sometimes within the first few minutes of play. The attacking element may consist of all the players ("High-diddle-diddle, straight up the middle!") or just a part.

Depending on the concept of the plan, attackers may divide into smaller groups. If a team is large enough to field an attacking force of 12 players, that force may decide to break into two groups of six, with one group taking one route toward the opponents' flag and the other group taking another. The decision to implement that or any other scheme must be based on such factors as terrain, the anticipated tactics of the opposition, the location of the other team's flag and the mental and physical condition of fellow players. In short, all of the factors in the *situation*.

No matter how many attacking elements there are, each one faces one of two choices: Go fast and noisy or go slow and quiet. Again, an analysis of the *situation* is important. For example, consider this Game field:

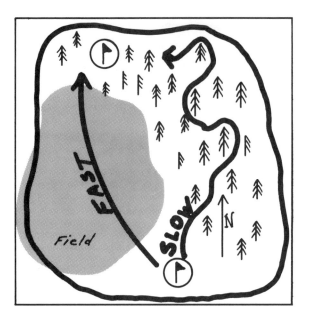

An attack element moving through the open ground on the western edge of the playing field might choose to go fast to minimize exposure. Conversely, an attack element moving down the east side might travel slowly and carefully to take advantage of the thick growth.

The most common error attackers make is falling apart on contact with the other guys. Either they break up into small groups, forsaking their goal of capturing the flag, or they mill around and do not attack. (A note is in order here. In almost any Team Game situation, lack of action leads to defeat. For example, if ambushed, a player should quickly retreat or charge the ambush, depending on how he assesses the situation. Sitting around or hiding, on the other hand, inevitably leads to a splattering.)

Ambushers straddle the defender–attacker fence. An ambush near the home flag is primarily a defensive posture. An ambush down in the other guys' land is offensive (as hell). Ambushers must realize that their job is to eliminate players on the other team, thereby reducing the odds. With that in mind, they must have alternate plans if opposing players do not walk into their ambush within a prescribed time. Otherwise, an ambush does nothing but tie up players who could be attacking a flag or defending their own ground.

Scouts scout. And they get shot a lot. But they serve several purposes. First, scouts can assess the other guys' defense without endangering everyone in the attacking element. Second, scouts can make the other guys think that the attack is coming from the left flank when, in fact, the attackers plan to come in on the right. Scouts, in other words, can be a diversionary force. You can read that as "targets," too.

Now we will put these elements together into brilliant schematics of possible plans. At the onset I will not say which plan I feel is the best because such information might compromise our nation's defense policy.

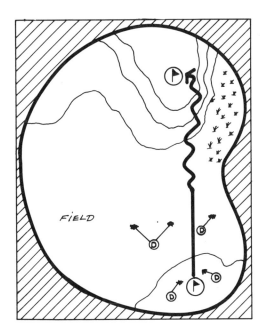

First, the situation. The other guys have 10 men on their team. We know nothing about their strategy. The field is shaped like a kidney bean with an open area on the left and thick woods on the right. The rest of the playing area is open woods. A swamp lies to the east. Our flag station is on level ground but close to the rear boundary, their flag is on high ground but approachable from several directions. Our team is singularly undistinguished.

We decide to keep it simple. We will leave a defense of four players and attack with six, moving down the right edge of the field to take advantage of the cover and to avoid the large open area. Initially, the attack element will run to cross the narrowest part of the field before the other team gets there, then the attack element will advance slowly on the flag. The defense will split into two teams with two players moving up to the edge of the field and two staying back to defend the flag. Simple, huh? Got it? Then on to something more complex:

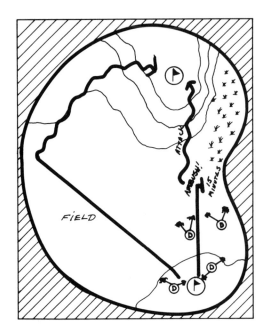

The situation is basically the same, except we know something about the other team—they like to run. Also, we have on our team four players under 25, who at least look as if they can sprint 100 yards. So we are going to get fancy.

First, we will set up the defense. Two players will hold back to cover the flag, just in case someone gets through. Two other defenders will move to the edge of the field, but they will shift more to the right (the east) than they did in the first example, because we think the other guys will try to dash in on our flag, and the quickest route would be down the east side of the field.

This time we also will send out an ambush element, four players who quickly will move across the field on the east side and set up, concealed and behind cover, on a line parallel to the other guys' direction of travel. The ambush element is assuming that the opposition will move between them and the eastern boundary, but if they are wrong and the opponents move past them on the west side, the ambushers still can splatter them merely by turning around (naturally, they must be camouflaged on that side, too).

The ambush element will hold in position for 15 minutes. If the opponents come through, they will let the first or second opposing player make a dash across the field, then pick off the remaining players. The defender on the edge of the field should be able to take out at least one of the players who gets through. The other one is trapped and should fall in time.

If the opponents do not fall into the trap within 15 minutes, the ambush element will become an attack element and move in on the flag.

The attack element of the four young, speedy players will run like mad to cross the western edge of the field. Once they are in the woods on the far side, they will advance on the opponents' flag slowly and carefully.

Whoopee! We win. Maybe. In any event, I cannot see a Game plan being more complex than that and remaining feasible. However, with a larger team there is the temptation to emulate a Patton or MacArthur or Rommel and try one of these.

The situation is this. Both teams now have 15 players. The opponents, all middle-aged, are considered partial to slow, cautious movement. Our team is much the same. Just smarter, of course.

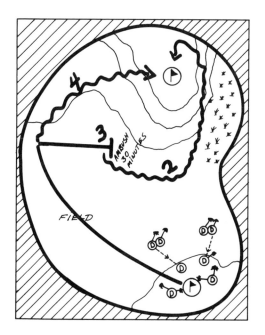

We will leave two players to defend the flag. With 15 players we easily can spare two for flag security. Four other defenders will set up two two-man ambushes at our edge of the field. If no opponent comes into their trap within 30 minutes of play, two ambushers will drop back off the field and take up defensive positions around the flag.

Meanwhile, the other nine players will move out smartly and cross the open area on the run at its western edge. Five players will drop off to the east. Three of them will set up an ambush. The other two will scout wide around the edge of the field and try to work up to the opponents' flag from their rear.

After 30 minutes of play, the ambushers, if unsuccessful, will break from their position and move in on the flag, following the route of their scouts.

The remaining four players will attack the flag from the west.

It might work, but I prefer "High-diddle-diddle, straight up the middle" myself.

There are a hundred—maybe a thousand—variations. That is what makes the Game interesting. If you would like to work out a plan for that same playing field, now is your chance. Here is the field.

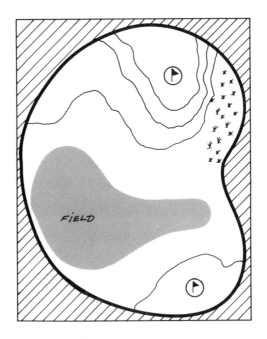

And here is the situation. Enemy: Six men, four women, all under 30. Terrain and location: Same as before. Friendly: Eight men, two women; six players over 30, one over 40, three under 30. Go to it.

Want the answer? Well, there is no answer! What do you think this is, some silly bridge column? You will have to play the Game to see if your plan works and if your players can follow your instructions.

Teams are the next smaller unit. In the Survival Game, teams usually are comprised of two players, sometimes three. Teams function together but within elements. For example, an attacking force of six players should be divided into three two-player teams.

Teams of two players are effective because there is comfort in numbers and because two players can do two things at once—namely, shoot at the bad guys and move in on them at the same time.

Teams are effective for two reasons. First, there is comfort in numbers. If you have to scout a flag location on your own, you are apt to chicken out about 100 yards downfield and go into hiding. But if you are with someone, you probably will keep going.

Second, teams can do two things at once, which one player cannot do. That ability is most useful when a team—two players—encounters the opposition.

It is called paint-and-maneuver, and it is the basis of any tactical movement. The premise is this. One good guy keeps the bad guy busy while the other good guy does something else, be it run for help, scream at the top of his lungs or move in on the bad guy. The first good guy keeps the bad guy busy by shooting at him again and again.

In most cases, the second good guy will try to work in on the bad guy and dust him off. Let's look at this quintessentially military maneuver on the big board.

Two good guys have penetrated the bad guys' defensive position and are closing in on the flag. But a defender lurks behind a log, positioned to hold off a rush. The good guys, working as a team, resort to classic paint-and-maneuver.

Good Guy A fires a couple of shots at the defender to judge the range and unnerve the villain. Then Good Guy A holds a steady bead on the defender as Good Guy B rushes to a tree (the rush should be no more than 10 yards). Should the defender show face or pistol, Good Guy A will shoot. He may not score but he will keep the bad guy down.

Now in decent painting range, Good Guy B fires on the defender while his partner advances from tree to tree, outflanking the bad guy and ultimately splattering him. The key to this tactic is maintaining

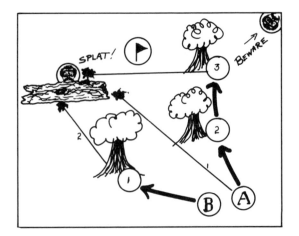

paint-pellet superiority. The more paint in the air, the less apt the bad guy will be to raise his head or shoot back.

One caveat: Good guys should be alert for other bad guys lurking about or stalking them from the flank.

An alternate strategy, and another attribute of teamwork, is the two-on-one rush. The attackers draw a shot from the defender, then rush him simultaneously. The defender may take out one good guy, but the other one should get him, then go for the flag.

A final thought is that two minds usually can come up with sufficient insults to goad the defender into charging. When he does, both attackers shoot him no less than 11 times for falling for the oldest trick in the book.

The *individual* is charged with simple guidance: Do not get shot, and if you do get shot, make sure you have taken out one of their guys. There is a whole chapter in this book on basic Game skills. They apply to the Team Game and should guide the Team player through. I've said it before and inevitably I will say it again: Doing something usually is better than doing nothing.

If you have stuck with me this long, you are serious about Team play, so I will let you in on some more refinements, namely that paragraph on *coordinating instructions*.

That is Armyese for doing the right things at the right time. In the Army much of it falls under the heading of S.O.P., a typical military acronym for Standard Operating Procedure, which means that certain things are done the same way all the time (but that makes a terrible acronym: C.T.A.D.T.S.W.A.T.T.).

If a team plays together enough, they will develop S.O.P. (plus B.O.). And they will run down the non-S.O.P. parts of coordinating instructions as a matter of course. But new Team Game players might improve their game by sticking closely to this list, which I will cover item by item, no doubt much to your delight.

Departure time is the time you leave. You know, like "in five minutes."

Formations and Order of Movement describe how groups move. The key to proper movement is not to bunch up and to put someone up front as a point man, so he can get splattered instead of you.

Routes and Alternate Routes outline the course you will take and the alternate course you might take should the first one not work. Remember that attacking elements will be going to the flag and then returning to their home flag. A hot team will route out both directions.

Rallying Points really are sophisticated. They describe the place folks

What to do at a danger area such as this road falls under the heading of standard operating procedure. Two players cover while a third prepares to dash across.

should go when everything goes wrong, which, inevitably, it does. Rallying points can give a team a second chance.

Action on Contact addresses what to do when the painting starts. Obviously, a larger group will attack, but a small scout element might opt for an alternate attack vector—that is, haul ass.

Action at Danger Areas simply tells players what to do when they come to a field or similar spot where they think they might get ambushed. The obvious answer is to be careful, and that means spreading out and sending a sacrificial lamb across first.

Action at the Flag defines what should be done when—wonder of all wonders—you finally get there. Does one player dart in or crawl in? Does everyone rush? Who will carry the flag back?

Finally, we come to **Command and Signal.** Command is decided by a flip of the coin or whatever other democratic method you might choose. If you want to play an organized game, someone has to be in charge and come up with a plan. Naturally, if you want to wing it, anarchy is OK.

Signaling in a Survival Game boils down to sign-countersign. What with everyone dressed in shades of olive drab, identifying who is the good guy and who is the bad guy can be a problem. So if you see or hear someone sneaking up on your flank, and you are not sure who that someone might be, give the old sign and wait for the countersign. Remember from war movies? It goes like this:

"Baseball." You say.

"Yankees." He says.

The question and answer obviously are coordinated before the Game begins. Be inventive. And remember that Japs have a hard time pronouncing "L" and Nazis never know who batted clean-up for the Red Sox in '42.

That's it. If you want to be a hotshot, here is another copy of my three-paragraph field order. You can cut it out, laminate it in plastic and carry it in your wallet. Of course if you're picked up by the cops on some minor charge and they find this, they will assume you are a whacked-out subversive. The only thing you will be painting for a while then will be borders on license plates.

1. Situation
   a. Enemy
   b. Terrain
   c. Location
   d. Friendly

2. Execution
   a. Concept
   b. Missions of Elements, Teams and Individuals
   c. Coordinating Instruction
      1. Departure Time
      2. Formation and Order of Movement
      3. Routes and Alternate Routes
      4. Rallying Points
      5. Action on Contact
      6. Action at Danger Areas
      7. Action at the Flag
3. Command and Signal

And one final note: If some absolute nerd somehow becomes the mastermind of your little team and he pulls out a dog-eared, laminated card and tells you what to do in a tactical synopsis that would make Karl von Clausewitz spin in his grave, just go along with the twerp until the whistle blows. Then do whatever you want to do—shoot the guy in the back, for all I care.

After all, it is only a game.

14

VARIATIONS OF THE GAME

As long as you wear goggles, we don't care if you hide in a corner and repeatedly shoot yourself in the foot. Variations give the Game spice. We soon may see Survival Game est, Survival Game marriage counseling and Survival Game autoeroticism.

Surely there will be Urban Survival Games played in abandoned buildings. The problem there now, as we see it, is informing the neighborhood, particularly the police, that the folks hurdling the rooftops with big, black guns are just hale and hearty fellows enjoying a bit of sport.

The fantasy of the Survival Game may be enhanced with Survival Game Pirates, played on sloops and schooners on the high seas; Survival Game Air Ace, played between small aircraft; and Survival Game Current Affairs, played between nations on remote islands such as the Falklands.

For now, however, variations of the Survival Game are but permutations of normal play. Here are a few examples.

Shoot-Out is a Team Game, often played at the end of the day. In Shoot-Out opposing teams face one another across relatively open terrain. The playing area may be outlined in surveyor's tape or simply described at the start of the Game ("this open field," or "the woods from the stone wall to the bottom of the field to the road to the pond"). Normally, the field for Shoot-Out is small. Five acres for 20 players is about right.

At a prescribed signal, teams converge and, like two British Squares engaging, shoot it out.

When one team eliminates the players on the other team, the judge may call out, "Free-for-all," at which point the remaining players attack each other. The last player left is declared Big Deal. If he or she has any sporting blood at all, he or she will spot the painted masses to a round of drinks. In some circles, Shoot-Out is called Climbing the Corporate Ladder. Instead of buying booze, the winner is expected to sponsor all the losers for membership in the local country club.

Secret Agent adds an interesting factor to a Team Game. Prior to the start of play, the judge selects one player from each team and secretly informs that player that he is a secret agent. The judge also gives the agent an armband from the opposing team. Only the agent and the judge

are privy to this information, but all players must know that Secret Agent is being played.

After ten minutes of play (I'll explain that time restraint momentarily), the secret agent may switch his loyalty from his original team to the opposing team merely by changing his armband. However, he may do so only once during the Game.

Where and when he decides to become a turncoat is up to the agent. He may find himself pinned down by an opposing player, and, in order to save a splattering, he may switch his armband—and loyalty. That is not a very effective move, however.

A more advantageous time to switch would be when the agent had four of his teammates huddled in front of him. He could slip off his band and possibly plug one, two or all four of them, then join the other team. Naturally, should one of those four players see the agent switching armbands, he would shoot the traitor. But that is the risk a secret agent takes.

If the agent is assigned to guard the flag station, he might switch his armband and attempt to take the flag. To prevent a secret agent from grabbing the flag at the start of the Game and running like hell before anyone is ready to play, the agent must wait those ten minutes before switching sides.

To succeed, Secret Agent depends on honorable players. A secret agent who switches back and forth from one side to another is a foul, loathsome, despicable, underhanded, slimy beast, who should consider a career as a real secret agent. Or politics.

Duels are inevitable. At the end of a Team or Individual Game, several people will not have fired their guns. Never fired a shot! Never had a chance to draw down that ugly Nel-Spot 007 on someone's guts and touch it off. Atrocious, really. All those healthy competitive urges will fester if there is no opportunity to pop someone. So the duel evolves.

The duel is . . . a duel. Two players, or two teams of equal numbers, gather in the middle of a field. Players square off back to back, and at a signal start walking. After a prescribed number of paces, they turn and fire. If players fancy historic convention, they will hold their ground and shoot—without moving—until someone is splattered. Most often, however, after the initial shot (which rarely scores), players run and dive and squirm over the field. Quite improper, really, but permissible.

Quick Draw is nothing more than a western showdown. You know, face each other 20 yards apart and say, "Draw, partner." The Nel-Spot is not the finest rig for slapping leather, but in a pinch it works.

The final variation is to use the old Nel-Spot to paint high ceilings, redecorate the living room or mark cattle, trees and telephone poles. Hmmm, that's a pretty good idea.

For those who have pellets and CO$_2$ left after a Game, the duel is most therapeutic.

Quick draw is nothing more than a Western showdown.

WHY, WHERE
AND WOW!

15

WHAT THE GAME IS NOT

Face it, your first reaction to the Game was tainted certainly with doubt, possibly with apprehension; I sure as hell know mine was. With its military trappings—camo, tactics and the gun—the Survival Game smacks of being a caricature of war. Since we Americans are raised to abhor war, our first response to the Game falls somewhere between *sicko* and *yuck*.

That reaction is normal and commendable. I do not argue with people who dismiss the Game with a shrug—and maybe a grimace—when they first hear of it. Americans are fighters, when need be, but we are not born and bred warriors who worship all things military. Thank God.

Those of us who have played the Game, however, quickly realize that what we are doing is not a parody of war, nor homage to it. For us, the distinction is obvious. The Game is play. The Game is rooted in fun, not in anger. Yet explaining that distinction to someone who has not seen or played the Game is difficult. It is hard because our disgust for the death and suffering in war is so intense that we condemn not only war but its most innocuous trappings. By association even the gear, such as camo, and the strategy, which is the same as that in chess or football, are dismissed as inherently evil things. I'll attempt to make a distinction between military trappings and war with this short tale.

I spent three years, four months and 27 days in the Army. For two years, three months and 27 days I had some good fun, supported at great expense by Uncle Sam. I launched a raft from a submarine. I rappelled down a building and out of a helicopter. I went camping for weeks at a time. I jumped out of airplanes. I played what even the Army calls games. There was some silliness in it, granted, and some unpleasantness and discomfort, but all in all those two years, four months and 27 days were good times.

Then I went to war for a year. In that war I learned one thing if I learned anything. The essence of war—the horrible aspects of war—had nothing to do with those two years, four months and 27 days of semigood times. Yes, we wore the same uniforms and moved in the same formations and tried to implement the same tactics we had used in those games in Georgia's woods. But those things were only military trappings.

And the trappings of war are not war. War is excruciating pain. War is fear so intense that men pray to die rather than continue to face that fear. War is hate, bred by that fear, so maniacal that sane men do insane things. War is death of a most unnatural cause.

Unfortunately, people who have not been to war as fighting soldiers—a group that includes many critics of the Game as well as too many politicians and a few generals—confuse the essence of war with its accoutrements. And when some military equipage appears in a game, critics jump to the conclusion that the game in some way must pay homage to war.

This game does not. The Survival Game may use military trappings, but so do marching bands, boy scouts, majorettes and football teams. What truly distinguishes the Game from war, however, is the atmosphere in which it is conducted. Fear and hate are the spirits of war; fun and camaraderie are the spirits of the Game. War is a terrifying reality; the Game is a grand, silly illusion.

Criticism of the Game goes beyond that obvious comparison. Often the gun is the focal point of voracious attack. That Game players point a

The Game is no more a homage to war than this pretty face is the face of a warrior.

big, ugly shooter at other players, then pull the trigger is interpreted by some to be a symbolic act of violent aggression.

The act is certainly an aggressive one. But the act of marking opponents with paint pellets is void of any intention of harm; it is aggressive but nonviolent.

Furthermore, the Nel-Spot is a gun only in the semantic sense. That is a more difficult point for many people to grasp. To people unfamiliar with firearms, a gun is a gun is a gun. Yet the Nel-Spot is but a long-range paintbrush, and everyone who plays the Game knows that. It cannot injure, as can a gun. Everyone knows that, too. And that knowledge is the key.

As long as players realize that the intent behind the gun is nonviolent, I cannot see reason to fear the gun or to equate it to a firearm any more than I can see reason to equate those smash-'em-up dodgem cars at carnivals to bloody car accidents. Granted, the gun looks ugly, but that appearance enhances the illusion of danger in the Game. So do open cars on roller coasters.

Further criticism of the Game often harps on two points: First, children should not be exposed to adults shooting at each other. Second, the Game simply is immature.

I will ramble again to answer the first charge. My four-year-old daughter has watched me play the Game. Naturally she was curious, and a bit confused, but I explained to her that the Nel-Spot was not a firearm, that it shot only marking pellets. Then I told her that the people running around the woods were not trying to hurt one another but were just playing a game. To her, the concept of adults playing a game is not all that strange. She watched the Game for a few minutes, then went about her business, which also is playing games.

I needed no further rationalization to play the Game in front of my daughter, but those who do might consider this point. I would rather see a child watching adults shooting paint pellets at one another and laughing than watching adults shooting bullets at one another and crying, which is the fare served up on TV these days.

To charges that the Game is immature, I plead guilty. But then on close examination so are most games. From superficial criticism to heavyweight analysis is a short step. On television the Game has been called everything from a "cultural lightning rod," to "a sign of these troubled times."

The Game will attract some weirdos—like a lightning rod—but I doubt if they will stick with it. There is too much silliness to hold the attention of hard-core fascists for long. And if attracting the deviant fringe is grounds for condemnation, then we must censure pizza parlors, bowling alleys and sports stadiums, too, because the types that hang around those places are often quite deviant. In the year and a half that the Game has been played, there has not been one reported incident of violence. Not a fist fight, not a shouting match. That is the telling point, for unlike most games, the Survival Game purges rather than feeds aggression in players and spectators.

A sign of the times? Not all that bad, I say. If frivolity and play are indicative of the country's mood, all the better. At least the Survival Game is healthier emotionally than cock fighting, public hangings, bare-knuckle boxing and pro hockey—forms of public amusement past and present that glorify violence and injury.

In truth, I don't think the Game warrants deep analysis. Certainly there are more pressing things to worry about than a game. The one

In the year and a half that the Game has been played, not one incident of violence has been reported. To the contrary, the Game is viewed by some psychologists as a method of purging aggression. The only violence at a Game is the inevitable attack on hot dogs following play.

psychologist who has studied the Game to any extent, Dr. Lester Mann of Penn State, says he finds "no evidence to indicate that this is the kind of thing that creates aggressive activities in people." To the contrary, Mann endorses the Survival Game as a healthy outlet for aggression. Although he admits a few of his professional colleagues have reacted with the same automatic revulsion one expects only in laymen, he notes that most psychologists either see no harm in the Game or express the feeling that "the jury is still out."

On the surface, the Game is easy to criticize. Yet among even the most voracious critics, few, if any, have actually seen or played the Game. Those who have most often say they find the Game silly. It does not capture their imagination. Such criticism I respect.

I feel the same way about golf.

16

BEYOND FRIVOLITY: THE
POTENTIAL OF THE GAME

No one looks for deep meaning in football. Play, fun and entertainment are sufficient to legitimize the sport. Why grope for more?

The same holds for the Survival Game. That it is fun, that it entertains people, that it does not hurt anyone is justification enough. The Game can stand on its own—as a game. Yet should one care to probe beyond those qualities, one may discover other attributes.

Good old American slap-your-buddy-on-the-back team spirit oozes from the Survival Game, so naturally organizations wishing to foster that feeling among their members have turned to the Game. Partners in law firms have played their associates. Executives have played fellow executives. An accounting firm has played a law firm with which it frequently works. Such groups unanimously have praised the Survival Games as a means of building esprit within their organization, enhancing bonding between members, even breaking down sex barriers. "For the first time I've been here, I really felt a part of the team," noted one female law associate after playing the Survival Game with her firm.

Several corporations have played the Game to expose their executives to stress in order to note how they reacted. A Canadian firm sponsored Games at its corporate retreat. A psychologist observed execs playing the Individual Game to see if he could draw parallels between players' strategies and their drive to achieve goals. Is a player who goes straight for a flag highly motivated? Is an aggressive Game player an aggressive businessman?

In the Team Game played by that same corporation, the psychologist wanted to see if individuals would function as a team or if they quickly would disband and proceed as individuals. No conclusions need be drawn from these events. They are noted only as interesting applications of the Game.

A firm specializing in career-performance training looks to integrate the Survival Game into its seminars. Reasoning may overflow with psychobabble, but certainly buried in the jargon—the physical-mental challenges, the self-realization and the body-mind training—is some validity.

In Rochester, New York, deaf children have played the Game. And had great fun.

Dr. Lester Mann, who edits the prestigious *Journal of Special Education,* is considering the Game as an outlet for aggression in hostile, emotionally impaired children. Notes Mann, "I am convinced that if we gave them the chance to shoot it out once a week, we'd quiet them down." Mann views the Game as "aggressive but nonviolent" and considers it a healthy catharsis for pent-up aggression and anger.

But what about you? Can you get something out of the Game, something other than a good time? When asked what they find rewarding about the Survival Games, players echo several themes, which, although not substantiated by psychological evaluation, certainly warrant a look.

The Game is self-reflective, and players are apt to play the Game the way they play life. Aggressive people play aggressively. Passive people play passively. Cautious people play cautiously. A player well might extrapolate Game performance to other stressful situations. Thus how you react in a Game may be an excellent clue to your behavior in the rest of your life.

A psychologist studied executives playing the Game to see if they played the way they worked. Is a player who goes straight for the flag highly motivated?

The excitement of the Game—the illusionary fear, particularly—heightens the senses. Players speak of feeling "really alive."

The Game provides the opportunity for players to experience immediately the consequences of their decisions. That is a noteworthy attribute in this age of "Wait a day or two and I'll send you a memo." In an article in *The New York Times* about white-collar executives who box for recreation, a psychoanalyst, who often counsels professional athletes, said he thought boxing appealed to men in powerful jobs because they enjoyed an "immediate experience," so often lacking in life. The Game provides that same experience, and without the risk of a restructured nose.

For many people, the fantasy environment of the Game is alien, and exposure to such a new experience can be illuminating. The element of fear, real or imagined, can be so pervasive that it may serve as an emotional and mental purge. Anxiety, hostility, aggression, paranoia—all that rotten emotional baggage—may be flushed out, at least temporarily.

You also may gain some new insights into others. Patricia Gaines notes that in her first Game she was paired up with a man of whom she was not particularly fond. But when the shooting started, she saw him for the first time in a different light. He was helpful, encouraging and concerned. Patricia left that Game with a new friend.

The excitement of the game—the illusory fear, particularly—heightens the senses. Players talk of feeling "really alive" and of experiencing great exhilaration.

Finally, the game is so infused with a sense of honor, camaraderie and fun that few players can walk away from it without feeling uplifted. Those qualities are very important in life, yet all too often are ignored. The Game focuses on them; that has to be good.

I could go on to argue that the Game is a way to get in shape, find a mate, resolve corporate takeover bids, develop those attributes that may lead to fame, fortune and a larger bosom, befriend cats, color one's parachute, shoot preppies, wear clothing from L. L. Bean, and maybe settle wars. But what is the point?

People who play the Game rarely need convincing to play again. And people who play the Game discover that if they want to mine the Game for deep meaning, the ore is there.

As for those who play because it is fun, I'm with you.

17

NATIONAL SURVIVAL GAME DEALERS

Since the Survival Game is still relatively new, what follows is only a partial list of places you can go to rent the equipment and play the Game. By the time you read this, there may be a field closer to your home. So please use this judiciously—it is subject to change. By all means telephone these dealers first for information and playing reservations. Although only a partial list, it should at least enable you to find out everything you will want to know.

NATIONAL SURVIVAL GAME DEALERS

Alabama
Doug Bowen
The Survival Game
Box 351
Madison, Ala. 35748
205-837-8406

Arizona
Jim Bertolani
Flagstock, Inc.
617 W. Grand Canyon
Flagstaff, Ariz. 86001
602-234-8624

California
William Beegle
The Game
Box 6053
Eureka, Ca. 95501
707-442-8950

William Bowers
Woodstock
Box 26435
San Jose, Ca. 95159
408-554-9298

Mike Denny
Bushmaster
8130 Firth Green
Buena Park, Ca. 90621
714-522-7044

Alec Jason
Bay Area Survival Game
Box 375
Pinole, Ca. 94564
415-864-1979
414-724-1003

Terry Hufford
The Challenge
Box 3870
Visalia, Ca. 93278
209-733-5493

The Bold Challenge
Box 2067
Tulare, Ca. 93275
209-686-9732

Richard Sinatra
Survival Sports, Inc.
1731 Howe St.
Box 254480
Sacramento, Ca. 95828
916-325-4685

Colorado
Dick Carmack
Survival Game Southwest Colorado
Box 2756 Hwy. 550-160
Durango, Colo. 81301
303-259-0026

Oscar Noel
Survival Sports, Inc.
Box Contract Station 3
P.O. Box 31434-2022
South University Blvd.
Denver, Colo. 80210
303-722-6653

Connecticut
Jim Iulo and John Poklemba
Survival Game of Connecticut
34 Stoneyhill Rd.
Brookfield, Conn. 06805
203-775-3494
800-952-9007 (for Conn. only)

Delaware
Michael Sharpe
SSL, Inc.
143 Wiltshire Rd.
Claymont, Del. 19703
302-798-1146

Florida
Ray and Phil Henderson
Competition Survival Games
Box 570427
Miami, Fla. 33257
305-251-6666

Jim Jackson
Survival Games of Ocala, Inc.
Box 128
Ocala, Fla. 32678
904-236-3245
904-629-8653 (pager #681)

Bob Griegs
Survival Games of Brevard, Inc.
333 East Merritt Island Causeway
Merritt Island, Fla. 32952
305-453-4770
(Field locations: Merritt Island,
    Tampa, St. Pete, St. Lucie City,
    and Indian River City.)

Jack Little and Bob Ruth
Central Fla. Survival Game
333 East Merritt Island Causeway
Merritt Island, Fla. 32952

Dave Smith
Mid-Florida Survival Game
474 Northern Durango
Ocope, Fla. 32761
305-877-2761

Georgia
Dennis Darnell
Survival Games of N.E. Georgia,
    Inc.
P.O. Box 2864
Gainesville, Ga. 30503
404-532-7362

Tom Jackson
Box 1218
Albany, Ga. 31705
912-436-5138

Hawaii
Peter Giordano
Orion Adventure, Inc.
1389 Queen Emma St.
Honolulu, Hawaii 96813
808-945-1065

Idaho
Woodrow Hassinger
Eagle Eye, Inc.
Box 370
Eagle, Idaho 83616

Indiana
Dwight Ferris
Southern Indiana Survival Game
3319 Larkspur Lane
Columbus, Ind. 47201
812-376-6004

Dennis Harper
Tri-State Survival Games, Inc.
P.O. Box 14969
Cincinnati, Ohio 45230
513-528-2585

Larry Bass
Box 247
Westport, Ind. 47283
812-591-3840

Kentucky
See Dennis Harper (Indiana)

Maryland
Tony Dent
Southern Maryland Survival
    Games
Lexington Park, Md. 20653

Maine
Mike Valente
Southern Maine Survival, Inc.
Box 1
Gray, Me. 04039
207-657-3436

Massachusetts
Peter Giordano
Orion Adventure, Inc.
79 Milk St.
Suite 1108
Boston, Mass. 02109
617-292-6400

Bill Griffiths
Minute Man Survival
452 Great Rd.
Acton, Mass. 01720
617-263-7366

Michigan
Mike Newbury
4629 10th St.
Wayland, Mich. 49348
616-877-9972

Bob Symons
Survival, Inc.
26145 So. River Park Dr.
Inkster, Mich. 48141
313-593-5792
313-277-8627

Larry Rathbourn
219 Lansing St.
Charlotte, Mich. 48813
517-726-1229

Minnesota
Dan and Jeff Holte
Twin Cities Survival Game, Inc.
5711 1st Ave. So.
Minneapolis, Minn. 55419
612-869-7916

Mickey Hunter
1802 Maplewood Ave.
Cloquet, Minn. 55720
218-879-3888

Missouri
John East
Rt. 1, Box 218L
Cape Girardeau, Mo. 63701

Nebraska
Bill Coch
118 Travis Dr.
Offutt Air Force Base
Offutt, Neb. 68113

Nevada
See Richard Sinatra (California;
   fields also in Reno and
   Las Vegas)

New Hampshire
Jack Walters
CHC
Carter Hill Rd.
Concord, N.H. 03301
603-225-4666
603-753-4733

New York
Jerry Braun and Ron Liquore
N.Y. Survival Game
Box 472
Armonk, N.Y. 10504
914-238-3525

Michael Cuocco
Survival Game of Long Island
266D Middle Island Rd.
Medford, N.Y. 14564
516-928-6489

Scott Smith
Corner of Park and Main
Cambridge, N.Y. 12816
518-677-2440

Caleb Strong
473 Benson Rd.
Victor, N.Y. 14564
315-223-9646
315-924-3583

Debbie and Bob Benedict
Great Escape East Survival Games
Box 546
15 Chapel St.
Sherburne, N.Y. 13460
607-674-9219

North Carolina
Dave Smith
North Carolina Survival Games
Box 52201
Raleigh, N.C. 27612
916-787-4756

Ohio
Cullen Demko
2228 Northland Ave.
Lakewood, Ohio 44107
216-221-0597

See Dennis Harper (Indiana)

Bob Netzley
Columbus Scouts & Raiders
   Survival Game
108 Imperial Dr.
Grahana, Ohio 43230

Oklahoma
Peacetime Adventures
Rte. 1, Box 134-C
Stillwater, Okla. 74074

Oregon
Bob Miller
Sierra West Adventures
4902 Portland Rd. N. #1
Salem, Oreg. 97303
503-393-2575

Pennsylvania
Mark Evangelist
Quest Survival Games, Inc.
182 Penn-Adamsburg Rd.
Jeannette, Pa. 15644
412-527-5946

Lester Mann
Challenges, Inc.
1950 Street Rd.
Suite 408
Ben Salem, Pa. 19020
215-646-2798

Les Robinson
Ponderosa Hunts
Box 3
Mountville, Pa. 17554
717-769-6902
717-285-5041

Dale Funkhouser
Survival Games of Conneaut Lake
R.D. 2, Box 1146
Conneaut Lake, Pa. 16316
814-383-2931
814-382-8686

Rhode Island
See Peter Giordano
   (Massachusetts)

Texas
John Carley
Texas Showdown
Box 5877
Austin, Tex. 78703
512-472-3540

David Evans
The Texas Challenge
Box 16572
San Antonio, Tex. 78232
512-496-1818

Utah
Peter Giordano
Orion Adventure
2004 South 800 E.
Salt Lake City, Utah 84105
801-584-2143

Vermont
Mark Lubanko
Vt. Survival Game, Inc.
R.F.D. #3, Box 160A
Chester, Vt. 05143
802-869-2674

Virginia
Grant Hagen and Barry Greif
1020 Poplar Dr.
Falls Church, Va. 22046
703-534-7011

Washington
Jim Moore
N.W. Survival Game
3924 E. 17th St.
Spokane, Wash. 99203
509-535-6076

West Virginia
John Simon
180C Rutledge Rd.
Charleston, W. Va. 25311

Wisconsin
Gregg and Brian Howe and Mike
   Moran
S.E. Wisconsin Survival Game
572 Pine St.
Burlington, Wis. 53105
414-763-5887
414-763-5085

Canada
Jerry Campbell
Eastern Ontario Survival
   Experience

133 Wilson Street West
Perth, Ontario
K7H 2P6
613-267-1015

Kai Gutheil
Blue Waters Survival Experience
909 Queens Ave.
London, Ontario
N5W 3H9
519-673-1838

Bruce Bleenkan
Toronto West Survival Game
896 Longfellow Ave.
Mississanqa, Toronto
L5H 2X8
416-271-0325

Steve Ingalls
London Outdoor Adventure
515 Grosvenor St.
London, Ontario
N5Y 358
519-439-3325

Lance Phillips
Vancouver Island Survival Game
c/o 101 Longdale Ave.
North Vancouver
British Columbia
V7M 2E7
604-922-7878

Rudi Perressini
Golden Horseshoe Survival Game
2753 Barton St. East
Hamilton, Ontario
L8E 2J8
416-561-0112

Al Symons
Pickerel Lake Lodge
R.R. 2
Burks Falls, Ontario
705-382-6447

Don and Jim Toner
West Coast Survival Experience
365 E. 2nd St.
North Vancouver
British Columbia
7L 1C6
604-986-0976

Rick Wall
55 Wynford Height Crescent
Apt. 2111
Don Mills, Ontario
M3C 1L5
416-444-3580

18

SING A SONG OF SPLATTERING, A POCKET FULL OF DYE

You gotta have a song, right? Butch and Sundance had a song. Bonnie and Clyde had a song. The Magnificent Seven had a song. CHIPs has a song. Everybody has a song, and we've got a song.

Our song is better than theirs, though. Besides, it ends this book on a happy note.

If you have never heard our song (OK, laugh, but it was part of the soundtrack on a what-you-call-your-major-network's coverage of the Game), this is how it goes: Dah dee dum, de de dum, dah dah dee dee dum. If you don't read music, call your favorite D.J. and make a request. If that fails, call the Survival Game and ask for Bob. He'll hum you a few bars.

The Survival Game Song

There's a game being played all across this land,
That'll test the courage of any good man.
It's based on the drive that keeps us alive.
In the spirit of revival the game's called Survival.

It began in debate when the hour was late
Whose skills would determine the wilderness fate.
Oh how the whiskey and words did flow
As three grown men took on childlike glows.

Each man wanted to prove and finally remove
Any shadow of doubt in this wilderness bout.
Whether dealing with thugs in the city streets or
Splitting wood for winter's heat
Whether R.F.D. endurance could whip mugging insurance.

Noel said in his southern drawl, "Nothing compares to a
    city brawl."
"On the other hand," said Gaines with a wink,
"I've got a C note that says it's instinct."
But Gurns in the corner never batted an eye.
He said, "Give me an hour, we'll see who survives."

The Survival Game Song

words & music by
David Seybold
& Bill Wightman

There's a game be-ing played all a-cross this land. That'll test the courage of any good man. It's based on the drive that keeps us alive—— In the spirit of re-vi-val The game's called Sur-vi-val.

It be-gan in de-bate when the ho-ur was late who's skills would de-ter-mine this wild-er-ness fate. Oh how the whis-key and words did flow—— as three grown men took on child like glows.

Copyright © 1982 by Great Legs Productions   New London, N.H.

At last a plan and after a year the game is now played
   far and near.
It's like Capture the Flag only players wear camo
And use guns that shoot paint-pellet ammo.

They smear their faces with grease paint brown, black and green
Dig it, baby, this ain't no country-club scene.
With their Nel-Spot pistols strapped to their hips
They stalk each other fully equipped.
The woods are thick and the hills are steep
And no player knows where the enemy creeps.

So yank your hands out of your Palmolive.
Finish your martini and eat your olive.
Park your clubs and your spikes in the garage.
No dues to pay just some camouflage.

Yeah, grab your Nel-Spot and CO_2
Prepare your mind, tai chi or kung fu,
Adjust your goggles then fix your beret.
Count your pellets now *vous êtes prêt,* you're on your way.

Some take to heart to criticize this game.
They pick it apart; they claim it's insane.
"It's not for us," the skeptics say
Until at last they finally play . . . the Survival Game.

Some people were really turned on.
They ordered their kits, blew a kiss to their mom.
Then off to the woods, to the top of the hills
To test their courage, fitness and skills.

Now lest we forget, we'll return to the nest
Of the founding three and their survival test.

It's a child's game played by adults
Using grown-up skills with amazing results
There is no bearing on status quo . . . yeah,
You know what you know.

The world of the sportsman, the wild and the tame
In the mind of the beast as he rustles his mane.
Your heart pumping strong alone and alive,
You take stock in yourself if you want to survive.

Well it's down to the wire over who is the winner.
There's a feeling felt by both vet and beginner.
Win or lose each player has passed the test,
And now he knows he's among the best
In a game that he played out in the wild.
A game that he learned perhaps as a child.
In a game, a game, it's called Survival, it's called
   Survival.
It's called . . . Survival.

—by Bill Wightman and David Seybold

The Survival Game Song © Great Legs Productions.
Reproduced by permission.
(Whom did you expect, Barry Manilow?)

JOIN THE SURVIVAL GAME ASSOCIATION AND FIND OUT HOW YOU CAN COMPETE IN *NATIONAL* COMPETITION.

State, regional, and finally North American competition in The Survival Game will begin soon.* To participate, a player must be a member of The Survival Game Association. For complete membership information and details on sanctioned competition, write to:

The National Survival Game
P.O. Box 364
New London, NH 03257

All members will receive:
    —Discounts
    —The Survival Game Newsletter
    —An Official Survival Game Patch and Membership Card

plus many other benefits.

---

*The first national play-off is tentatively scheduled for the fall of 1983. Prizes will be awarded and the finals will be televised.